The Best Cellar

The Best Cellar

Jeff Smith

Volt Press
Los Angeles, California

09 08 07 06 05   5 4 3 2 1

Library of Congress Cataloging-in-Publication Data

Smith, Jeff, 1960 Mar. 6–
    The best cellar / by Jeff Smith.
        p. cm.
    Includes bibliographical references and indexes.
    ISBN 1-56625-242-3 (alk. paper)
    1. Wine as an investment. 2. Wine cellars. I. Title.
HD9370.5.S63 2005
332.63—dc22

                                                        2005010718

Volt Press
A division of Bonus Books
9255 Sunset Blvd. #711
West Hollywood, 90069

Printed in the United States of America

For Donnie and Joe

Contents

Introduction: The Iceman Cometh

I did not consciously decide to become "the wine cellar guy." As a young man I had no intention of getting involved in the wine industry, except perhaps at the business end of a glass. Nothing about my early career path suggested it would culminate in me becoming the organizer of other peoples' "liquid assets," or an occasional refrigerator salesman. And yet, here I am and I couldn't be happier about it.

For good or ill, I owe my start in the wine business to my father, Joe Smith. His passion for collecting wine dates back to the early '60s, before doing so became fashionable. He is also a raconteur of some renown, and his stories of wine collecting have taken on a legendary stature over the passage of time. When he was an executive at Warner Bros. Records, he went to London on business and was entertained in grand Continental style by his counterparts from the English company. On his return, he went to Greenblatt's, a liquor store and deli at the eastern end of the Sunset Strip and told Roy Kavin, the owner, that he'd had this great wine called Lafite-Rothschild. "Have you heard of it?"

"Yeah, I've heard of it."

"Can I get some?"

"We just got their latest vintage in, the 1961."

"Great. How much is it?"

"Four dollars and seventy five cents a bottle."

"That sounds pretty steep."

"Take a case home. You'll be glad you did."

And so, if any of this can be believed, he started his collection by buying the equivalent of a Babe Ruth baseball card.

My own love of wine started at an even earlier age. As a kid of eleven or twelve, I'd bike to the local wine shops to see if they had any B.V. Private Reserve (also called Georges de Latour). I was a pimply-faced kid, with a squeaky pre-pubescent voice, and I probably made quite a sight as I asked the liquor store-owner if I could use the phone to call my dad to report that the store was carrying a hard-to-find Cabernet.

As a teen my knowledge of wine made me stand out even more. When I was sixteen, my girlfriend's parents took us to a really fancy restaurant for her birthday. To everyone's astonishment, I asked the sommelier to see the wine list. The drinking age then was eighteen, but I looked about twelve trying to wrestle with the enormous leather-bound book. I ordered a "precocious" Trefethen Chardonnay and suggested that the 1970 Clarets were "drinking well."

I suppose I knew more about wine than other kids, like which wines were first growths and that Leroy and Jayer were very desirable Burgundies in good years. I knew certain names like Chateau St. Jean and Martha's Vineyard and so on, but if I learned one thing about wine from my father, it is that wine is meant to be shared with people who can enjoy and appreciate it with you. I don't know all that much about its chemical properties, but I do know that introducing wine to a meal can turn an evening out into a memorable event.

None of this explains how my father, Joe, got me into this mess. In 1997 my parents moved to a new house in Beverly Hills complete with a beautiful cellar they had built by Jean-France Mercier. After the movers unpacked my father's collection and put it away Joe called me to see if I would help him do an inventory. And that, friends, is where our story begins.

Of course I was going to help him, but first I had to figure out *how* to help him. Joe's got around 5,000 bottles in two different cellars—upstairs and downstairs—with hundreds of titles from different regions and vintages, each in a unique cellar location. And all of it was already put away in slots. It was a nightmare of organizational logistics. A wine cellar is not a record collection. You don't simply slide the new Abba album in the front of your milk crate and just move the others back one. A wine cellar is a messy place.

I talked to a numerous wine store-owners about how they kept their inventory, and the consensus was that a Microsoft Excel spreadsheet could accomplish most of what I wanted to do. I didn't know that there were a dozen software programs available and anyway I didn't want to use a complex program that I was then going to have to teach my father how to use—especially after he'd only just mastered how to send an e-mail.

One rainy day we went to work. My father stood on a stool, calling out the names of the wines with as much detail as he felt was necessary to find them again, moving left to right, from numbered column to numbered column. I dutifully recorded every bottle, and when it was complete I printed the inventory out in both alphabetical and vintage order by region, and filed it in a beautiful leather notebook embossed with the word "Wine" in gold letters. It was, and is, the best-read book in his house.

A few years later I did the same for my brother-in-law when he built a new cellar. A friend of his asked if I could do the same for him, and Carte du Vin began its first tentative steps. My brother-in-law's friend paid me five hundred dollars to inventory his three-hundred-and-fifty-bottle collection and I had a revelation: "This guy paid me five hundred bucks and he doesn't have any wine. Imagine what this service would be worth to someone with a real collection."

My sister said, "I think there's a business here."

"And besides," I told myself, seeing a light-bulb go off overhead, "I don't have a job."

Worlds are turned on such notions. I printed up some business cards, hung up a shingle and started Carte du Vin Wine Cellar Management. We specialize in inventorying existing collections, and helping clients to improve their collections by guiding them through the process of buying and selling wine. As I learned more about wine and developed better systems for organizing it the quality and efficiency of Carte du Vin improved. In less than a year, I had clients in six states and feature stories in the *Los Angeles Times* and the *Wine Spectator*.

At the time when the light bulb went off, I was writing the follow up to my worst-selling (as opposed to "best-selling") humor book, *Life Sentence. The Best Cellar* is not my planned sequel nor is it a book about wine, per se. There are plenty of those. This is a book about wine cellars and the people who own them, based on my experiences with Carte du Vin. I will try to spare you any mention of the weather in Burgundy, yields per hectare, or the history of oenology from Biblical times. Instead *The Best Cellar* will guide you in building a wine collection, show you how to store it properly and enable you to keep track of your investment so you can enjoy it more thoroughly.

I love what I'm doing—all day long I work with people who are passionate about the great pleasures of life: wine, food and travel, and who can argue with that? I love having created a tiny niche for myself in this world, a little business opportunity that seems to have legs. I love wine cellars and the mysterious treasures that lie within. Now, wherever disorder rules the racks, wherever people live in fear of the mess in their cellar, wherever wine cries out for justice, I'll be there.

1

Why a Wine Cellar?

In my world, the reasons for cellaring wine are so abundant and obvious, that it is simply a given that one would want to have a wine cellar—I've never had to convince a prospective client of the necessity of building one. My business is built entirely upon the notion that my clients will have reached that conclusion already.

While the reasons are myriad and complex, it can be boiled down to this: older wines taste better. They become more valuable over time. Wine lasts longer when stored properly. With older, better, more valuable wine being properly stored at hand, you will win friends and influence people. When you show off your worldly sophistication by sharing your treasures, it will make you appear taller and more handsome. Everyone will want to have sex with you. And it will be really, really great sex.

But enough of the soft sell.

Storage

At some point you're simply going to need a place to put the stuff. Back in ancient times, when my father got started collecting, he kept the wooden Bordeaux cases in the closet of the maid's room in the back room of the house. They were stacked up five or six cases high on either side of her sad little closet, leaving just enough space for the poor woman to hang a single white dress uniform on a single wire hanger. This was my first experience with something we wine snobs refer to as "indifferent cellaring."

The best solution is to have a cellar in the house. Some people have whole rooms dedicated to their collections; others convert a closet under the stairs. In either case, these rooms tend to fill up quickly—nature abhorring a vacuum—and a larger space is soon required.

Several of my clients keep their collections in lockers at wine storage facilities around town. These temperature-controlled warehouses provide optimal conditions, but are often inconveniently out of the way. Once there you usually have to shuffle around your boxes to dig out a certain bottle. Storage units are useful as a stopgap measure, or for deep storage for new wines that you don't plan to drink for some time.

Smaller collections can be kept in special wine refrigerators that maintain the temperature and humidity. My own Vinotheque (the refrigerator brand name) is now insufficient to house my growing collection, which I like to think of as "small but mighty." When confronting this same problem, some people will ask: "What should I do?" The answer is: "Move to a bigger house with more wine storage capacity." Voila! Problem solved.

Choices

If you have less than two hundred bottles you probably don't need to construct a cellar unless it's going to be a showpiece in the dining room (a "cellar" being a state of mind, not a room in the basement). Otherwise you're better off getting a special wine refrigerator and be done with it. But as soon as you designate a dedicated space for your collection in your house you'll discover the pleasure of taking a short walk to the cellar and choosing a wine for that evening's meal, or to take to a restaurant or dinner at a friend's house. Locker guys* have to plan out their consumption a week in advance. So much for spontaneity.

Having a cellar also means there's a good chance you won't run out, and that may be justification enough.

Pride of Collecting

At some point, there are only so many things you can really go ape over. If you're lucky you've got a couple of teams you root for, a political candidate who inspires passion, a family you love, your golf game or ski trips, and then what? A great car is still just a fancy way to get around town; a wine collection is a lifestyle.

The reason people become passionate about wine is that it is the

....
*I will refer to people as "guys" or use the masculine throughout the book. There is no slight intended; it's just simpler than doing a he/she or him/her in the name of political correctness. All but one of my clients are men.

ultimate confluence of nature and technology, art and science, earth and the elements, romance and commerce, man and God. And it tastes good, too.

When you love wine and collecting, the bottles are your babies. I like to think that having your own Carte du Vin (the wine inventory list I make and will explain step-by-step how to do yourself) is like having a book full of baseball cards—except you own the team. You're George Steinbrenner, and they're the Yankees. Making the call for a bottle at dinnertime is like tapping one of your players on the bench to go pinch hit with the game on the line, "Now get in there son, and show 'em what you've got." The question is do you put in the untested rookie, that coltish Aussie who promises power, or the wily veteran who's been a solid performer, even if he can't hit the curve ball as well as he used to?

There is no better hobby than collecting wine. Not stamps, not coins, not watches, not cars. Maybe art. Cars are good too. But ultimately wine brings people together like nothing else. It is a hobby that lends itself to a shared experience, full of expectation. Popping the cork on an older vintage is like letting the genie out of the bottle. A great bottle of wine can turn an evening into an event, a meal into a lasting memory. And, of course, you can't drink coins.

A reporter for ABC Television asked me "How much of wine collecting is just about showing off?"

I told her, "27 percent."

There is an aspect of wine collecting that has something to do with showing off. It's not so different from other types of collections that display a pride of ownership, and a dedication to a pursuit whose goals are luxury, taste, refinement, and enjoying the finer things life has to offer. To the victors go the spoils. A wine cellar is a statement that says: "Look what I've got." (Other peoples' cellars say: "Look what I don't got.") It doesn't define the collector, but it speaks to his personality and his character. And besides, it ain't bragging if you can back it up.

Provenance

Many collectors will argue that a lesser wine, properly stored, will drink better than a finer wine that has not been well maintained. Auction catalogs often make mention of the provenance in particularly florid terms. Here's an example from a recent Christie's catalog: "Removed by Christie's staff from a fastidiously maintained temperature and humidity controlled home cellar. The dedication to the optimum storage conditions and the search for the very best bottles are without bounds. This collector bought only direct from the chateau or the most assured sources and shares his passion freely. Purchased with connoisseurship and cellared with ultimate care." Wow! I'm sold.

The tent-poles of proper wine storage are: a cool and constant temperature, controlled humidity, low light and low vibration, and adequate ventilation and insulation (more on these later). Keeping good wine in less than optimal storage conditions is as regrettable and avoidable as leaving a convertible in the rain with the top down.

Puttering

If you are still unconvinced about the wisdom or necessity of building your wine cellar consider this: no one will bother you in a room that's fifty-five degrees—a wine cellar is the last refuge for the modern man.

There's almost no end to how much time you can spend in your cellar looking at all your junk, deciding what to pour that evening, or just gazing at your holdings and congratulating yourself on how daring and clever you were for buying these babies in the first place.

We have a friend who has flatly refused my offer to help him organize his cellar. He loves going down there to get a bottle, and for him part of the fun is the thrill of rediscovering a forgotten treasure in his racks.

A wine collection is one of the great clock-killers of all-time.

Gifts

I have one cousin who doesn't drink, but this hasn't stopped him from acquiring some very good wines that he likes to have on-hand for entertaining, and to use as gifts. Many years ago, when he still drank, he bought 1990 Bordeaux futures. Their value eventually increased 500 percent, outpacing the stock market, and he was in a position to give them away as gifts—including a Haut Brion for my wedding.

Once you've become known as a wine collector, people will expect you to bring a bottle of something special wherever you go. My wife Amy's Great Aunt Sylvia invited us over to a family dinner, and Amy sent me an e-mail asking if I would bring a bottle.

I sent back a terse response that read: "No. Just because I'm some kind of 'expert' am I expected to bring a bottle to every family function? No. A thousand times no. I won't hear of it. Is Paul (our brother-in-law, a bankruptcy attorney) bringing a legal brief with him? I'm sorry, but the answer is no, I will not bring a bottle of wine to dinner tonight. I'll bring a magnum."

Wine guys are invited everywhere.

The flip side of this is that no one ever wants to bring a bottle of wine over to a wine snob unless they're sure. They're petrified of screwing up. The only bottles I ever get are either great bottles meant to impress or those brought by wine-challenged people who have absolutely no idea: B.V. Coastal. "Thank you," I say with a grin, and then I put them in the closet marked "cooking wine."

Learning

As hobbies go, wine is a lot like sports. There's a lot to learn, and that's part of the fun of it all. Every winery is like a sports franchise.

Wineries play in a league, either that of the region or the type of wine, and most leagues have divisions (appellations).

There is an owner, of course, usually a colorful rich guy or a gentleman farmer, sometimes a group of shareholders or even a major corporation. (Nobody likes the corporate teams.)

The wine maker is like the coach or general manager. He (or increasingly, she) is responsible for taking all the disparate elements and weaving them into a cohesive whole.

The vineyard is like the stadium or arena where the team plays. The hectares and yield are like the seating capacity of the venue.

The terroir, the soil composition, the vines and rootstock are, collectively, the franchise history. Every franchise/winery has a history. You come to expect consistent results from each team, year in and year out. The Clippers are never a disappointment, because we never expect anything from them. If the Lakers have a three game losing streak, however, there is cause for concern. (There has been much cause for concern of late.)

The growing season is the pre-season. So much is determined by decisions that are made before the team ever takes the field.

Harvesting the grapes is the opening day of the regular season.

The advance notices on barrel-tastings are the pre-season predictions in the newspapers. These handicaps are daring, controversial, sometimes predictable, sometimes surprising, and almost always wrong to some degree, and, like odds-makers, they often set the prices.

Each vintage is like the team from a different season. (Unlike sports, however, in a good vintage, almost every team wins.)

The elements are the positions. The weather, the amount of rain and sunshine and fog and wind, the temperature and ripening through the summer, are variable from one season to the next, like the players. Collectively these elements form a team with a Win-Loss record. Sometimes these players complement each other, coming together in a magical combination for a championship season.

"Second labels" are minor league franchises.

The journey from the vineyard to the bottle to your cellar is the playoffs, where the end result is forged by the winemaker/coach's preparation.

Buying a bottle from the new vintage is like drafting a player out of college.

Opening and tasting each bottle is like the finals—best out of twelve. If you missed everything else, this is the time to tune in to the show.

The price is the score.

The scores are the stats.

The tasting notes are the post-game recap.

You start to learn this stuff. You become a knowledgeable fan. You know that a certain winemaker used to play for another team before going into free agency. You get a feel for the game. You compare teams from different eras. Unlike sports, however, you can sometimes put a fantasy match-up together and let them fight it out in the glass. A vertical of a great wine is like seeing the '72,

'82 and '02 Lakers playing a game of round robin. Wilt vs. Kareem vs. Shaq.

Liquid Assets

Highly rated, high end wines that can improve over time are a better investment bet than most mutual funds. As wines grow to maturity, those that are properly stored in temperature-controlled settings will generally become more valuable. (Let me offer this one caveat: If you want to make a little money trading in wine . . . start with a lot.) Most wine shops charge a premium for older vintages, so the best financial advice is *buy early & hold 'til maturity*.

Recently I ran into my old boss from the St. Regis at the hotel bar. I told him about Carte du Vin and he said it was a good idea but that he didn't need my services because he knew where every bottle in his cellar was.

"Really? How much wine do you have?" I asked.

I knew that this guy had a remarkable memory for figures. "Around 3,000 bottles," he said.

"Around? Is that plus-or-minus 10 percent?"

"Sure."

"Okay, Fred. I know what kind of wine you buy. 10 percent would be around three hundred bottles, which at an average price of one-hundred-and-fifty-dollars per bottle adds up to forty-five thousand dollars of wine that may or may not be in your cellar. That's like saying you can't find a Mercedes Benz in your living room."

I told this story to a mutual friend of ours named Larry, who in turn described a recent evening at Fred's house. Apparently Fred was climbing all over his cellar searching for a specific bottle for dinner until finally Larry said, "Come on, Fred, just grab a bottle and let's go—we're late for our reservation."

My company, Carte du Vin, is predicated on two notions: I believe that once you've hit a critical mass of around one thousand bottles in your cellar, you don't really know exactly what you've got, and that, after a certain point, you don't know where it is, either. The defense rests.

In addition to being a hobby and a passion, a wine collection is an investment. A wine cellar is, literally, a liquid asset. A big part of the reason people build a wine cellar is to protect that investment. A lot of wine goes bad, or gets consumed before its peak, or is simply neglected because people aren't watching their portfolio. I often work with clients who would never allow their gardens to be overrun with weeds, or would refuse to drive their car with a warning light blinking on the dashboard, but regularly allow an equivalent level of neglect with their wine collections.

The appraisals I provide are used for legal valuation (estate planning and divorce) and insurance purposes. Most homeowners' policies cover only 10 percent of the value as "unscheduled personal property," provided that you have an inventory of what was lost in a disaster.

The price of a bottle of wine is something about which there is a great deal of speculation and fluctuation. It is a commodity that is sold at auction, so the price one pays depends almost entirely on when, where and how they buy it. Recently I found out that an old work colleague was going through a divorce, so I sent a brochure to his office and suggested that I could get him an appraisal that was favorable to his cause. I followed up with a couple of calls that went unreturned, so I sent a second brochure to his wife. I'm like an expert witness; I can make the case either way—just make sure you get to me *first,* before your estranged spouse does.

When I provided another divorcing client with an appraisal—at the low-but-reasonable end of the spectrum, he told me that he "gave it a haircut," shaving 15 percent off the total before submitting it to his wife's attorneys. They took the appraisal out to a well-known sommelier for his assessment. The lawyers came back and said that they thought it was about 15 percent too low. (I loved that one!)

There are other reasons why you may want to know the value of the wines in your collection. One client had me separate his wine into areas on a wall designated by price. On the left were his pretty good wines, the least expensive of the lot, which he shared with women-friends. These were his "chick" wines. On the right were the serious wines, the impressive names, the big-bucks bottles. These were his "guy" wines. He wanted to make sure he wasn't wasting the good stuff on a chick that might not know the difference. (As an unanticipated consequence of this fiendish plot, there are a lot of guys who want to sleep with him.)

2

The Elements of Proper Cellaring

The key elements to cellaring wine are fairly straight-forward and simple. A cool, constant temperature is important. You don't want direct sunlight or a great deal of vibration. Add a modest degree of humidity and adequate ventilation; keep the bottles on their side (or upside down, if you must), lock the door, and you've got it. Thanks very much for buying the book—I'm outta here. Good night.

Cool Temperature

The precise temperature at which wine should be maintained is widely agreed to be fifty-five degrees. Science was never my strong suit, but take my word on this; I looked it up. If you want to spend time and money learning about "ullage" (the term for the airspace between wine and cork) or "temperature oscillation induced expansion" in a real book I can't stop you. It's your funeral.

The reason you want to keep the wine cool is that it retards spoilage. It's the same reason you see fish kept on ice in the market. That much science I understand. I don't know how fifty-five got to be the magic number, but it is. A few degrees in either direction ($\pm 3°$) won't kill you, although the temperature will affect the rate at which maturation occurs. More than a couple degrees cooler might "numb" the wine so that the flavor never fully recovers and the wine will not evolve as well as it might otherwise. More than a couple degrees warmer and the aging process will be accelerated in unfortunate ways and the evolution of the wine will be awkward. Hot is bad. When I buy wine from out-of-state brokers during the summer, I ask them to hold off shipping them until the weather cools off. (The same theory applies to shipments in the depth of winter.)

I have a good friend named David Wyler. I'm using his name here to set an example for others. On more than one occasion he has shown up to lunch or dinner with a bottle of wine he's been storing in the trunk of his car. In Los Angeles. In the summertime. This is yet another unfortunate instance of what is meant by "indifferently cellared."

The best self-contained refrigeration units are Whisper-Cool. They are widely considered by professionals to be both the best engineered and to have the best service. A bottle probe gives an accurate temperature reading of the wine inside the bottle on a digitized LED display. Breeze-Air is the other leading manufacturer of compact cooling systems, and was considered the Rolls Royce of refrigeration units until recently. After 1,500 square feet you'll have to consider a commercial system sized to the room and duct the system with all the equipment in a separate room, or on the outside of the house, connected by Freon lines.

Constant Temperature

If you had to choose between a somewhat higher constant temperature of sixty degrees and a cooler but fluctuating temperature, take constant. Variations in temperature are the greatest enemy to wine except being exposed to air. Temperature fluctuations can cause the cork to expand or contract and ultimately let air seep in—and that's bad. This is known as a "weepy" cork, and I weep along with it.

If you take a wine out of the cellar to the refrigerator, drink it. If it's white wine, keep it in the refrigerator and drink it next week. If you don't drink it and put it back in the cellar, don't freak out about it—most wine will survive. It's not the best thing for the wine, but it probably won't kill you or the wine. Just don't do it again.

In colder climates you may need to consider a heater to keep the temperature constant if there is temperature fluctuation in the house, especially in older homes.

Humidity Controlled Environment

Once again, I'm going to try to "demystify" the science of wine storage for you here: Wines age more slowly under moderate humidity than otherwise because dry air will allow wine to evaporate through the cork. My exhaustive research (I asked a guy who said he knew) confirms with absolute certainty that a humidity level of around sixty to seventy-five percent will prevent wine evaporation without allowing mold to form (which may ruin the labels).* Of course there is another side to this argument. A prominent cellar builder told me that the humidity issue is "Pure 100 percent bullshit." According to him, the relative humidity in most climates (excluding Palm Springs and Las Vegas) is above 50 percent—indeed in some beach areas the issue is about removing humidity from the cellar. He finished up by telling me that the humidity argument originated in European wine rooms that are always damp in an effort to prevent what's known as "the angel's share," namely the evaporation of up to 15 percent of the wine from inside the barrels.

I suggest getting a Thermometer/Humidity gauge (a "hygrometer" or "humidistat" to you pedants) from the Wine Enthusiast, IWA, Brookstone or elsewhere—some hardware stores carry them. If your cellar is more than twenty-five hundred cubic feet, get two and place one at either end of the room to see that you're getting both a constant temperature throughout, and an even level of humidity.

Low Light

After exposure to air and heat, light is the next biggest enemy to wine. We're not entirely sure if it's the light itself or the heat, but ultra-violet rays will penetrate even dark green bottles, creating a series of unpleasant chemical changes. If you're building a cellar, make sure to provide adequate, discreet lighting, keeping in mind

....

* Hugh Johnson suggests "A coat of varnish or a squirt of hair lacquer is a very useful protective measure against the sort of moderate damp that will cause mildew to form on labels over a period of years." But he cautions that a dripping crypt is not a place to collect wine.

that this isn't a library and a wine label isn't a novel. Don't use fluorescent light. Use dimmers and smaller wattage bulbs that cast off a warm light. Less is more. Halogen H-99 units are good. Ideally the lighting should create a nice atmosphere but only a little heat. Rope lighting is good for the display rows as they throw off almost no heat. (In any event, the amount of heat produced has less of an effect on the temperature of the room than your own body heat.)

Here's another clue for you all: Don't buy bottles you see in store windows.

Low Vibration

While there is not a lot of scientific study on the subject, vibration is widely thought to be bad for maturing wine. Fortunately, vibration is not a major problem most people have to overcome in their wine storage choices. If you keep away from subway platforms, airport landing strips and discotheques, you should be fine. Also, never juggle with filled wine bottles.

All kidding aside, by using individual bottle racks (one or two deep), you limit your exposure to loss due to earthquake. This may not seem a major problem to most people, but the restaurant Valentino in Santa Monica lost nearly two hundred and fifty thousand dollars of wine in the 1994 quake. Owner Pierro Selvaggio said it looked like "a river of blood" flowing down the stairs of his restaurant.

(There is a sweet ending to this cautionary tale: Pierro had been so influential in introducing wine, and especially Italian wine, to Southern California, that several of the top producers, including Gaja, sent him cases of wine to help make up for his losses.)

Californians may want to consider earthquake-proofing their cellars by covering open bins with doors—keeping in mind that you have to be able to move around in the cellar with the doors open. Ben Benoit of Cellar Masters uses rubber footings on his racks that damp out some of the vibration and, even though the filled racks have a lot of weight, nothing is fixed to the floor.

Part of the reason you don't want a lot of vibration is that it stirs up the sediment that collects in the bottle. It's a good idea to remove a bottle from storage at least a day before you plan to pour it, especially if it has some age on it and some sediment in it. Real pros have a nifty decanting machine that places the bottle at a forty-five degree angle and allows you to gradually pour from there without stirring up the gunk at the bottom ("Gunk" is trade terminology we professionals use).

Adequate Ventilation

Much as I like the romantic notion of a musty "cave" (say it with a French pronunciation: *cahve*), the truth is that we live in an age of electricity and the exhaust from the refrigeration unit has to go somewhere. This is usually a good time to tell the contractor, "Figure it out."

Insulation

"In practical terms for a householder," Hugh Johnson begins, "the most important factor is insulation." Let me skip the detailed explanation about "temperature gradients." Basically what it means is this: you've got to keep the good (cool) air in and you've got to keep the bad (hot) air out, and the more insulation the better.

You will want to have a vapor barrier and insulation for all the walls, floor and ceiling if you build a cellar in the house. Different builders have different theories about the placement of these barriers. One explained to me that he puts vapor barrier on both sides because it's so inexpensive to do, but another uses a vapor barrier only on the warm wall, arguing that moisture gets caught between the drywall and the insulation. Moisture is bad.

It's better to use rigid insulation if you can, because fiberglass can get wet and become ineffective. Ask a lot of questions about it. Toss in the term "temperature gradients" and see if it gets a reaction. If not, you're talking to the wrong nerd. In the long run, proper insulation will pay for itself in reduced energy bills because your cooling unit won't work as hard. (In addition, the temperature of a properly insulated cellar won't change more than a couple of degrees in the event of a power failure.)

Bottle Position

There is a reason that wine is stored on its side. What reason, you ask? I quote the great Hugh Johnson: "Store all wine prone so that the liquid is in contact with the cork." Got it? Keep the cork wet and the seal tight. When you store a bottle of wine standing up, especially in a dry atmosphere, you risk losing the spongy resilience of the cork in as little as a few months, allowing the dreaded enemy, air, to gain a foothold.

If you're keeping your wine in open boxes—first of all, why are you keeping your wine in open boxes?—place them in the box with the neck down and the punt facing up. This will keep the cork moist and allow you to say, "punt."

Security

I grew up in a house filled with wine. Occasionally my friends would suggest that I take bottles out of the cellar (which was in the attic for a while) for our personal consumption, with the idea that Pop would never know they were missing. I did not do as they suggested. Well maybe once or twice, but the point is that having a lot of wine lying around can be an incredible temptation to others, including people who come to work in the house. (Hey, that's me!)

My father had a famously bizarre break-in at our old house. He'd relocated his cellar from the attic to the retrofitted pool house cabana in the back yard and one day went out to find the doorjamb broken and five cases of the oldest and rarest wine missing. Whoever did it knew what they were taking. A ransom note, with the cryptic message: "You will have no wine before my dime," was left behind.

No ransom demand followed. My dad sent out faxes to all the major auction houses listing the wines stolen from the cabana. If they came on the market, someone would know.

A couple weeks later, Gordon, a business associate of my father's, got a call from a friend who handled estate sales, saying there was a bunch of old wine being offered for sale and did he want to buy it? Gordon had a look at the wine list and guessed that they might be my dad's stolen bottles, so he called Joe's office to see what he should do. My father was out of the country, but he passed word back to Gordon that he should try to buy it back.

That Friday afternoon, Gordon gets in touch with the seller who arranges a meeting at the end of a secluded street above Mulholland Drive in the Hollywood Hills. He's told that it's for sale as one lot, for eleven thousand dollars. Cash. No cherry picking. (The wine was valued at three to five times as much).

Gordon scrambled to put his hands on the money before the

banks closed and got a friend to go with him, in part because he was afraid that he was going to be mugged for the money by what appears to be, at best, an unusually unscrupulous wine merchant.

So off they go, very cloak and dagger, in Gordon's Bentley to meet the fence at the drop. When they arrive, there's a guy, nervous, driving a real piece of shit Nova in need of a paint job. After what I'm sure was a brief introduction ("You the guy?"), he opens the trunk. There, alongside the guy's greasy towel, tire iron and a basketball, are fifty priceless bottles, all jumbled together in the wheel well of the trunk. For sure, Sherry-Lehmann does not conduct business this way. Gordon and the friend ask if they can open a bottle to see if it's still good, and the guy agrees. They go back to the Bentley and pull out a corkscrew and a couple of good crystal glasses they'd brought with them, and open a '45 Lafite. It was just fine. So they paid the guy, put the cork back in the Lafite, backed up the Bentley, transferred the wine from one trunk to the other, and went their separate ways.

Joe got his wine back, the insurance company was thrilled they only had to pay out on the price, not the value, of the wine, and everyone was happy.

The next week a team of security people installed an alarm system and a custom grate that could've kept Willie Sutton out. Let that be a lesson to you: put a lock on the door.

3

Cellar Construction

Mea culpa: Until very recently I had never built a wine cellar. But, increasingly, I'm called in to consult on wine cellar construction. One cellar builder practically spat at the client who asked for my help, "What do I need him for? I've been in this business for twenty-five years!" Yeah, bub, you have, but I spend more time in wine cellars than anyone I know. I actually know how people collect wine, and what they're going to need. These considerations will help determine how much space you'll need, and how much you need to spend to accomplish your goals.

There are other books on the subject of wine cellars, but they're all terrible. Feh. Believe me, gentle reader, you're not going to want to read another book about wine cellars after you've put this baby down—I read them, so you don't have to.

Building a Cellar

SCALE

Wine collecting is not a rational hobby. One client explained: "The fact that I have more than I can possibly drink in my lifetime is totally superfluous."

The first thing you need to consider is scale: how much wine you've got, and how big you realistically think you're going to grow your collection. The rule of thumb is that the size of the cellar will dictate the size of the collection, but you shouldn't let the lack of space hinder your rabid consumption schedule. It is an inherent law of physics that nature abhors a vacuum. My father would argue that it is a mortal sin to have an empty slot in your cellar while there is even one more bottle of good wine to be bought in the world. Think big. The bigger the better. One client built a nice little cellar off the dining room but had most of his stuff stashed in lockers where he couldn't get at it. Then he lost one hundred and ten pounds (his wife) and built the cellar he needed to house his growing collection.

Jean-France Mercier, one of the wine-cellar builders to the stars, says that when you are planning to build a cellar, you should, at the minimum, double the amount that you already own or plan to acquire. One of my top clients is adding another *room* onto his sixty-five-hundred-bottle cellar. Nobody ever lamented having more space than they needed. Believe me when I tell you that someday, somebody is going to need you to hold on to their wine for them.

My friend and client Michael is parking some wine at my father's house right now while his cellar is being built. Aim high.

The next thing you need to consider is how you use wine in your life. I have one client who feels guilty about opening a whole bottle with dinner. His wife doesn't drink so he only has a glass or two, and it is agonizing for him to have to pour half of a good (or great) bottle down the drain at the end of the night. The answer? Half-bottles! I recommended six cases of good (and great) 375 ml bottles to him. Ornellaia, Ducru, Montelena. Finally he was happy, except that he didn't have any racks that would hold the smaller size bottles, so we ordered a little insert that retrofit the racks to do just that. If the cellar builder had asked for my input (what do I need him for?), I would have strongly suggested that a few rows of racks should be able to accommodate half-bottles. They're perfect for dessert wines. My experience has been that most people can't or don't like to drink a full glass of dessert wine. (They don't know what they're missing, but that leaves more for me.) In that case half bottles will do the trick and the smaller format means they'll age more quickly, which, in this instance, is very good news indeed. (The reason half bottles age more quickly and large format bottles age more slowly has to do with the amount of air in the bottle as a percentage of the size of the bottle.)

Not everyone is a fan of the small-but-mighty 375. Hugh Johnson says, "In theory the slightly faster maturing speed of a half-bottle should allow one, effectively, to peer into the future of a long-aging wine. In practice the wine in half-bottles is unlikely to give either an accurate or encouraging picture of the larger bottles."

The same is true at the other end of the spectrum: large format bottles. Everything from Magnums to Nebuchadnezzars are going to need special treatment. They're impressive looking, so make sure you allow some storage space and, importantly, some display space just for large bottles. One client of mine has an island in the middle of his cellar just for oversized bottles. He's got one bottle, a Nebuchadnezzar (fifteen liters, or twenty bottles in one) that has its own case. It outweighs my seven-year-old nephew, Max, and is taller than his four-year-old brother, Jack. (A word of warning: when opening a bottle larger than a magnum, have two people on hand to decant, and make sure you have enough decanters to do the job.)

CUBES

Another client has a large collection made up of cases of Cabernets, Italian reds and Bordeaux. However, he also has a significant number of "whatever" bottles: single bottles, gift bottles and odd bottles. These random bottles always seemed to wind up on the floor, or sadly in the way somehow, so we had some "cubbies" or cubicles built for them.

I know this seems like a small thing, but if you get cubbies/cubicles made, make sure they're big enough to hold between twelve to eighteen standard sized Burgundy bottles nested in rows of four or five. A client who ignored my advice, and built his cubes to hold eleven Burgundies, wishes he had listened to me. (Bordeaux bottles will also fit in a cube measured for Burgundy, but Burgundy bottles do not necessarily fit in cubes measured for Bordeaux). You may want to have the cubes constructed on a slight bias so the bottles are leaning with their weight against the back wall, making sure the corks are wet.

DIAMONDS

I don't like diamonds. There is an old-world association that goes with them that appeals to some people, but they're not the best way to store wine. The mass of weight rests on a single bottle, causing an inherent instability. Furthermore, the Burgundian bottle shape is not meant to be stacked, so they are even less stable. If you install diamonds you will always want the bottle that's at the bottom. If you really must, use diamonds for your party wine or everyday wine that you buy by the case, not the good stuff.

The most common bit of advice I give to people building cellars who plan to use either diamonds of square "cubbies," is to make sure they hold twelve bottles comfortably. Wine still comes in cases of twelve, so a diamond that holds eleven bottles is not helping you.

CASE STORAGE

My brother-in-law has started buying in case lots. It is embarrassing to admit that we now have a problem about what to do with all the wine he's bought over the past several years. The racks he installed are full to overflowing, and each new case is a challenge to put away. I designed an island unit similar to something I've seen in stores, with one bottle on display and room for eleven more of the same underneath. It added storage capacity for another 528 bottles, gave him a countertop and finished the cellar in a beautiful way. (We love countertops.)

A lot of people like to keep their wine in the original wooden cases. It looks nice, it's better for reselling, and it keeps the light out. Make sure to allot enough space for boxes. Eurocave makes a very smart case racking system that allows you to keep the wine in the original wooden case, using the least amount of space. (The Eurocave Classic Roll Out Racks—available through Wine Enthusiast.)

As a general rule, keep the case storage at or below chest level, as it's hard to safely handle cases above that. Make sure the case storage is deep enough so that (a) you can position the Bordeaux cases with the printed side out and (b) it makes for a natural counter-top if you have single-depth racking above. (We love countertops.)

ODD-SIZED BOTTLES

Some bottles, such as Champagne, Zinfandel, and some Burgundies and Rhones, don't fit into standard Bordeaux racks. I've seen countless bottles of Dom Perignon and Krug and Turley with shredded labels after being jammed in, and yanked out of too-small racking. (A torn label does not alter the wine inside, nor does it significantly change the perceived value of the bottle, according to the auction houses. Even so, enjoying wine is a sensory experience, and part of that is the aesthetic appeal of the label.) As the great Durante would say, "What a revolutin' development!" Do you need larger racks? Yes, you probably do. Bring this up with the designer when you're drawing up the plans. Some racking is variable, allowing for more than one size of bottle to fit comfortably.

THE DOOR

One of the biggest problems with wine cellars is the door. Hot air from the house can come through the cracks if you don't treat it like an exterior door with weather seal or sweeps to keep the cool air inside. My cellar door has double-thick insulated glass.

THE TASTING ROOM

Several of my clients have tasting rooms in or adjacent to the cellar. Here's some good advice: don't put your dining table in the wine cellar. It's fifty-five degrees in there and women wearing open-toe shoes tend not to enjoy it. Furthermore, at that temperature the wine never gets warm enough for the bouquet to open up, and the food you serve will quickly become too cold to enjoy.

Better to build a small room outside the cellar where you can store all the wine junk—giant decanting devices, framed lithographs with vinous themes, the big bottle full of old corks. The most common accessories in the tasting room are old, empty bottles, sometimes signed by the winemaker or guests from the dinner where it was poured. If a wine cellar says, "Look what I've got," these relics cry out: "Look what I've *had.*"

THE COST

Wine cellars aren't like paving a driveway, where you measure the square footage and figure out the material costs and do some fast math. All cellars are custom built, from the size and dimensions of the room to the design elements, the racks, flooring, ceiling, lighting fixtures and doors. The look is important, but so is storage and you have to strike a balance between the two. Always keep in mind that what makes a great cellar is the stuff inside.

A good contractor who knows what he's doing with regard to insulation, refrigeration units, etc., can do the job. A wine cellar specialist might cost more, but will do it right the first time. Of course, we're all in cahoots, so you can't trust me.

For those hearty, foolish souls who endeavor to do it themselves, there is a book of dreary prose, but good advice, titled: *How and Why to Build a Wine Cellar*, by Richard M. Gold, Ph. D. You can find it on Amazon.com. I personally think you're crazy, but good luck.

Freestanding Refrigerators

Recently I got a call from an actress who wanted to discuss building a cellar at her modern home in Santa Monica. I took one look at her modest collection of Colgin and Bonaccorsi, and said, "What are you, nuts? You don't want to build a wine cellar in here. You don't have any wine." I waved my arms for emphasis. Then, like Burgess Meredith in the first *Rocky* movie, I told her, "What you need is a refrigerator." And so I added refrigerator salesman to my resume, fulfilling a lifelong ambition to provide properly chilled beverages to a hot and thirsty world. (My grandfather used to claim that he "could sell ice in the wintertime." I sold an ice-box in the wintertime. He would be so proud.)

Caveat Emptor: Every wine refrigerator on the market has less real storage than the amount they quote in the advertisement. You'll want to see if you need more shelves than the basic model has, and other extras like a glass door or a veneer finish will run a few hundred bucks each. My favorite brands are Eurocave and Vinotheque, which run ten to twenty dollars per bottle. Less expensive solutions are available at around six dollars per bottle (see www.westsidewinecellars.com).

If you're planning on getting a wine refrigerator for the kitchen, the best built-in brands are Traulsen, Sub-zero and Viking, all very good looking, very efficient, and very expensive. Eurocave also makes a less-expensive under-counter unit.

Lockers

Many of my clients have such large collections that they are obliged to store some in wine storage facilities. I spend a lot of time at these facilities, working on my clients' lockers. I keep the wine for my Liquid Assets group at a place called the Wine Hotel. Twice a year I go in and sort everything out in time for our shareholder's dinners. I find it very relaxing, almost spiritual. I put on my iPod and get into it. (Yes, it's true—after working in cellars all week, I occasionally go and do it *for fun*.)

I love consolidation, and in a locker consolidation is essential. Space is at a premium, and you're literally paying by the square inch, so make it count. In your locker, you will want to make sure you get eleven or twelve bottles in each case. Throwing out an extraneous box at the end of an organizational session is pure joy.

The advantages of keeping your wine at a storage facility is that it's safe, it doesn't take up a room in your house, and the storage conditions are going to be flawless. The disadvantage is that you can only get at your collection during business hours, and any visit requires planning which ends any spontaneity. There's a wonderful line from the movie *The Sure Thing*: "Spontaneity has its time and place." The problem is that you probably have your wine stored in boxes, stacked one on top of the other, and the bottle you want is inevitably in the bottom box.

To get around this inevitability, I've begun installing metal shelves on castors in lockers. Costco sells them for around seventy dollars per set, and using them means you don't have to stack the boxes more than two or three high, and you have easier access to the entire collection.

The Alternative

The alternative to all of the above is "don't worry about it." That's the advice from Dorothy J. Gaiter and John Brecher, the two nincompoops who write the Tastings column in the *Wall Street Journal*. First of all, they spend most of their column inches suggesting twelve-dollar bottles of wine to their well-heeled readership. It would be fine for the local paper, but theirs is probably the most desirable demographic of any publication in the world, and they never seem to think anyone would want anything better—like good wine for instance. They seem to love everything—Blue Nun, Riunite, you name it.

Giater and Brecher recently ran a story that quoted a 1934 book called *Wines: How, When and What to Serve*: "No sharing of a coal bin, a kitchen, or a wareroom will do." (They keep most of their wine in a closet with a relatively stable temperature.) They further suggest that you get a little refrigerator to keep a few bottles at fifty-five degrees, because "that's the temperature where we most enjoy both reds and whites."

Storing your wine in a coal bin is horribly wrong, and so are they. If you want to enjoy the bouquet then fifty-five degrees is just too cold for a red wine. That's why people take their wines out of the cellar before serving them.

Fortunately, wine people don't take this kind of advice seriously, or I'd be out of a job. Frankly, I hope the Gaiter-Brecher's never ask me over to share one of their poorly kept grocery store wines. (And with the period at the end of that last sentence, I'm pretty sure I don't have to worry about it.)

Ode to an Empty Box

If anyone had told me in my youth that one day I would seek out and covet certain empty boxes, I would've told them they were nuts. Now I freely admit it. I spend a lot of time with boxes, and there are certain boxes that I hold above all others. I could write a song about the cardboard White Burgundy box, two extra-wide layers of six each, separated by molded inserts, contoured for your pleasure. I buy them for a buck apiece wherever I can. People in the know hoard them like pieces of gold. I've got seven of them in my garage at this moment and two more in the trunk of my car. They hold the most wine in the least amount of space and can stack up to about ten high without getting wobbly. You don't have to pull out any nails, or reseal them with nails if you want to reuse them. They are glorious.

First runner-up is the classic wooden Bordeaux box, with

grooved slots and wooden inserts with the shape of the bottles carved out. If unopened, you can stack these, one on top of the other, all the way to heaven. The tops tend to fall apart and have to be nailed back down in pieces, but these are great. (Taking a hammer and nail to shut a case of '75 Petrus can be a rather nerve-racking experience—a job I gave to my new assistant on his first day.) Of course, most of the "new world" wines come in insanely odd-shaped bottles, which are either too wide at the base or too tall to fit into either the cardboard White Burgundy or the wooden Bordeaux boxes. Whose idea was that? I'm convinced there's a glass guy making a mint selling crazily shaped bottles to winemakers who are desperate to get noticed.

Almost everything else in the box world is crap. Insulated shipper boxes are only good for shipping because they take up too much space in the cellar or locker. They cost about seven dollars each when new, but you can't give them away at the wine storage places. If you need to ship wine, my advice is: go to the storage facility and offer the guy a buck apiece for his empty shippers. The only other good thing about them is that all the crazy new bottles will fit in them.

You can't stack the garden-variety cardboard Cabernet box more than three or four high—but you can look in from the top and see everything, so there's value to that. Occasionally I pick up a case of wine in one of these cardboard boxes, four rows by three rows, with the top cut off. What kind of sick person cuts the top off a box? Call me a box prima donna, but no top, no love. Forget it. Can't go there.

I've now taken to buying my boxes in quantity directly from the manufacturer. I learned the hard way that you can't just pop over to the liquor store on Saturday morning and pick up one hundred boxes to pack up and move someone. I also have some strong opinions about tape. One might reasonably ask, "What is there to say about tape?" Beneath the seeming simplicity of taping a box is a mystery unfolding. Wasn't it Richard Feinman who said, "Everything is interesting if you look closely enough?" I spent a day putting an auction parcel together with a specialist from Sotheby's, and it was like watching a ballet. He was an artist with the tape gun, the Picasso of adhesive. He used more tape than anyone I've ever seen, the mark of a true professional boxer. "Tape to tape," he explained with a shrug. His boxes were gorgeous. I would know his work anywhere.

Tape is cheap, but don't use cheap tape. I bought some stuff at Staples, thinking I was getting a great deal, except for one thing: it didn't stick to cardboard. Whoopsy-daisy!

4

How to Make Your Own Carte du Vin

Let's assume for a moment, gentle reader, that you have already bought into the rationale for having a wine cellar. Let us further assume that you are interested in cataloging your vinous treasures. If not, I suggest you skip ahead to chapter 5.

I'm going to give away all my secrets in the next few pages. I'm going to explain exactly how I prepare a professional Carte du Vin wine cellar inventory, from start to finish. I'm going to do this because I want to live in an ordered world. Hopefully, when I'm done, I'll still have a job.

Before you get started, full of good intentions and an ardent desire to see order come from chaos, you have to understand that a wine cellar inventory is never completely right. With that in mind and forewarned, read on.

The Wine Doctor's Kit

When I started doing this, I used to show up with a laptop, power cord and a pen. I'd have to rummage around in the client's kitchen looking for a screwdriver to open up a wooden case. Over time, I put together a kit which I now use all the time. If you plan to do this yourself, it's a good idea to keep a complete kit in your cellar or locker. At some point, you'll need everything in here and, except for the hardware, the whole deal will cost about the same as a bottle of the current vintage of Opus One.

ACOUSTIC:

Flathead screwdriver or crowbar
Hammer and nails (1″ with flat heads are best)
Packing tape and dispenser
Marker pens in different colors
Blank Address labels (mixed sizes)
Scissors
Label maker
Extra label-maker tape cartridges
Pens
Legal pad or scratch paper
Clipboard
Mini first aid kit (bandages, Neosporin, Advil)
Empty notebook with ½″ ring binder
Towel
Paper
Plastic page sleeves

Tape gun

Corkscrew (you might get thirsty)

Dry hand wash lotion (wine cellars are dirty places)

Trash bags

Gloves with sticky material*

ELECTRIC:

Laptop computer (with power cord, external mouse)

Extension cord

CD-RW discs

Flashlight

Portable printer**

Extra ink cartridges for printer**

Getting Started: The Grid

Before you start a-counting, you will need to do a few things. Firstly you'll need to create a numbering system on a grid. One nice thing about most cellar collections is that they are basically made up of columns and rows, and/or bins, which all form a square-ish grid. I use a label-maker, but you can have nice ones made by a carpenter or go to a trophy shop and get some metal plates made with adhesive backing.

Columns are listed as numbers. I try to put the labels at eye-height, beginning with Column One at the far left as I enter the cellar, then continuing left-to-right.

....

Optional. One of my assistants loves them, but I'm on the fence and my other assistant won't wear them. Wine cellars are dirty little places and gloves definitely keep your hands clean and unscratched reaching into tight, double-deep racks—but I don't know that they improve your grip, and they make it hard to type.

**Not strictly necessary if you're going to print out elsewhere, but very, very cute.*

If there are bins, label them B1, B2, etc., from left to right, to set them apart from the single or double-bottle racks.

You want the labels to be visible but not obtrusive to the eye. Ben Benoit of Cellar Masters hides his on the inside of the column so you can see them only if you know where to look.

Run the alphabet from top to bottom. Generally, the ceiling in the cellar is uneven, so you have to find the highest point where a bottle is stored and label that A. If there is a display rack, it should have the same letter throughout, regardless of the top letter in the column. You'll want to have enough alphabets running down so you can easily find them, but the room shouldn't start to look like an eye chart.

This process is, without a doubt, the most mind-numbingly dull activity I engage in at Carte du Vin.

A Place for Everything & Everything in Its Place

My sister sometimes asks when I became such an organized freak. I'm not sure I agree with her characterization, but it could have been the summer between high school and college, when I worked in a record store. I was an absolute phenom at putting records away in the racks, from Abba to ZZ Top. People would call me to come help them sort out their album collections at home.*

I'm a little obsessive and a little compulsive, but not enough of either to qualify for a disorder; in fact, disorder is the problem. I like to think that I have obsessive/compulsive orderliness. I will ask

....

* As anyone will tell you, Jethro Tull goes under J, but Alice Cooper goes under C. Taj Mahal is a stumper.

if you want the bottles wiped down or if you'd prefer to keep the dust on them to show their age (as many restaurants do). The point is that you will want to be organized and methodical in this endeavor. (It will also help if you can type well and spell accurately in other languages.)

My father and I have been having a good-natured debate on the merits of alphabetization for several years. I'm for it, he's against. I am well organized, he is poorly organized. You decide.

Most of the time, I have a brief consultation with the client before we get started. I ask them how they've got the cellar organized, where they plan to grow their collection and where they're starting to taper down. More often than not, they think they've got it all together. Then I tell them that whatever system they were using is now a thing of the past. The times they are a-changin'. "You're in my house now," I want to say.

Move 'em Out

The process of creating a beautiful, functional Carte du Vin cellar is akin to making a sausage: You don't want to see how we do it. When I first started doing inventories, I would get up on a stool and start counting at 1-A, move down to the bottom of that column, then start over in 2-A, all the way across, and then try to make sense of it on the computer.

Not any more. Now we come in like a swarm of bees. We take a cellar apart and put it back together again the way we like it. The first thing we do is move things out. Lots of them. If preparing a wine inventory were a military operation, this would be the part called *Clearing the Area* or *Securing the Perimeter*.

First we empty out the cellar, one area at a time, figure out ways to create more space, and then fill each area back in maximizing the efficiency and usefulness of the overall cellar. In an optimal situation, the cellar has a table where we can line bottles up and work on. If there's enough room in the cellar, we empty out a whole section and move it all over to one corner. If there's no room in the cellar, we move the contents out into the hallway or adjoining room. Some people get a little freaked out and I nearly always hear something like, "Is the wine going to go bad? Isn't it bad for the wine to change temperature like you said in the other chapter?"

Yes and no. Look, this stuff used to live outdoors in a variable climate. Then it was in a huge room at a certain temperature. It's been on trucks and boats and more trucks. It's been in warehouses and stores before you ever laid hands on it. Not all of them were refrigerated to precisely fifty-five degrees Fahrenheit. The point of keeping your cellar chilled and at a constant temperature is to retard spoilage. The wine inside the bottles is hearty stuff. It will survive a couple hours outside the temperature and humidity controlled cellar. Be cool, man. I'm not killing your children. Not yet. We'll get to that later.

One big rule: close the door. You're going to have to keep it open some of the time, but if you're not schlepping things in and out, keep the door closed and the cold air in.

Now the organization begins. We want to get all the like kinds of wine together. Bordeaux over here, Burgundy there, Cabs, Varietals, all down the line so the cellar intuitively makes sense when you walk in and look at it. The Carte du Vin book will probably follow the same layout.

Next we "shuffle the deck."

I am yet to work in a cellar where everything was really lined up correctly. At some point, your new Moutons didn't fit with the old ones, so they got themselves into a place we think of as "over there." Some of the Moutons are "over here," but the others are "over there." Shuffling the deck is a bit like the old television game show "Concentration." If you can match up this one with another one of the same, you'll win a prize. Maybe an Amana Radar-Range Oven. Who knows?

Within each part of the cellar, we like to group the same producer and same wine together. It's nice. It's neat. It makes for an attractive display. When you've got all the different years of a producer lined up in the same column, it's literally a "vertical."

Sometimes this is a bit like playing a life-size game of Tetris, trying to make everything fit just so without knowing how many pieces you've got. It helps if you have a good sense of spatial construction.

Occasionally we get pretty deep into it, only to find that we're going to run out of room for something. Then it's time for what we call the "Student Body Left," named after the play that helped win O.J. Simpson the Heisman Trophy. You can't run this particular play unless you've already "Moved 'em out," because you're going to need to put them somewhere.

Software

There are quite a few wine inventory software programs on the market. They have slightly different features but are basically all pretty good and will handle anything you need. In fact, I find that they all do a little more than what you really need. I don't need to annotate most wines by country of origin or color. I don't see the point of it, but they fairly insist on including this information. You can buy any of them with confidence for twenty to fifty dollars. Or you can take one minute to create an Excel spreadsheet that does about everything that the others do for free. (Lots more on this in a minute.) Some of the better ones are:

- *Vinote:* this program was developed by a New Zealand rancher who had to keep track of unruly animals. He turned his organizational skills into a hobby, then into a business.
- *My Wine Collection*
- *Cellar!*

The worst, by far, is Robert Parker's *Wine Cellar Manager.* I love Parker[*] but his cellar software sucks the big one. Everyone I know who has tried to use it finds it incomprehensible; I'm in the business, and I have no idea how it works. The bells and whistles on this program just make noise. I developed a headache that I thought was a brain tumor trying to use it and from what I can tell, no one has ever figured it out. It asks for all kinds of useless information, and forces you to build a virtual wine cellar. However, the program does have a lot of the tasting notes, scores and (unreliable) prices you can access pretty easily.

The problem I have with all the software programs I've tried is that they tend to ask you for more information than is necessary to get the job done. I know that Bordeaux is in France. I know that Chardonnay is a white wine made of Chardonnay grapes. If you decide to work with one of these programs make sure you can pre-configure it to only ask you for the pertinent information about every bottle.

....
[*] *I've met him once, and he is an amazing guy. You can argue all day with his ratings, with his love of highly extracted wines, but you cannot fault his integrity, his knowledge and his place in the annals of wine journalism and wine appreciation. He is the most influential critic of any kind in the world today, and I stand in awe of him.*

Be the Guy

The most important quality you need to successfully inventory your wine collection is will. You need to get on the ground, on your hands and knees, you need to stand on your tiptoes on a step-ladder to reach the bottle at the top, to laugh at the splinters in your hands, and to stay in a room that's below sixty degrees for hours and hours at a time. (I'm probably the only guy who brings Capilene ski clothes with me to Las Vegas in August.) Software won't do any of that for you. You still gotta get your hands dirty and do the damn thing. Software doesn't type.

During the summer a new client asked me to come look at his cellar; he said that he was pretty well organized. In fact he was thinking of just doing the job himself. I pointed out that Kistler Chardonnay probably did not belong in the middle of his red Burgundy section and that I wished him well, but that he should say good-bye to football season. That was in early September. By early October, he was thrilled to be paying me to get it done.

The problem with organizing your own cellar is that almost anything will provide an adequate distraction from the task. This particular client works long hours at his job, and he wants his wine cellar to be a retreat from all that, rather than more hard work. The words, "Honey" and "Daddy," or the possibility of spreading out in front of your high-definition plasma screen on your day off, instead of freezing your ass off, rolling around the floor of your basement, can provide a real strong inducement to hire me. The guys I work with are like butlers—they walk into a room and look for work. We work fourteen-hour days with a thirty-minute lunch break. There's nothing else.

Get a Guy

If you're going to do this, get another guy. Two guys working together will finish the job three to four times faster than one guy working alone. Get a guy who knows about wine and doesn't mind freezing his ass off, rolling around the floor of your basement. You may want to pay this guy, because your friends will leave you before the job is done.

It may sound a bit pedantic to suggest that the person you hire for this project should know something about wine, but there's a lot of information on that little label, and the bit in two point type that says something like "Le Rocche dell'Annunziata" may be the difference between a thirty dollar bottle and a two hundred dollar bottle from the same producer. It matters, and guys who collect this stuff pay attention to these not-so-little details. The vineyard designation is not always prominently placed, nor is it in the same place from one label to another. You need to know to look for it, and you need to know to ask for it, so it helps if your assistant knows something about wine. One of my guys was a sommelier at a restaurant. Another worked in a wine shop. They know how to handle the stuff.

One tip about working in the cellar is to hold on to those bottles tightly. I've handled over a million bottles and out of those only three have broken, but I didn't drop any of them. (For the record: one fell on my head, another fell between the slats of a shelf—a design flaw, and the third got knocked over on an uneven concrete floor. Even so, that's not a bad batting average.) If you're working with a guy, pass the bottles with all due caution. (I carry a one million dollar insurance policy because all I do is move expensive, breakable stuff around expensive homes filled with other expensive breakable stuff. I hope I never have to file a claim, but I like knowing that I can.)

Excel Tutorial

Warning: If you *are not* in the process of composing a Carte du Vin, or seriously considering making one in the immediate future, I cannot urge you strongly enough to skip this chapter and pick up the book again with chapter 5. It's really dreadful stuff, but you decide.

Further: If you *are* in the process of composing a Carte du Vin, templates of the various Excel pages described below can be easily downloaded from my Web site: *www.thebestcellar.com* and select Templates from the menu.

Recently I was called by a prospective client who said that I had given his friend, an existing client, a great inventory software program. We talked some more and I showed him about all the specialized programs on the market, and then I showed him how to hack one out himself by using Excel. Microsoft Excel is loaded on just about every computer in the world. It's not terribly difficult to learn how to use, and it's pretty intuitive if you're familiar with computers. There are books available with titles like, *Excel for Utter Morons* with lots of pretty pictures and step-by-step checklists. I am pretty much that Moron, so I bought one of these books and learned how to do some of the more complex stuff. For the purpose of this book, I'm going to give you a summary of the major points: (Note: the instructions that follow are for Excel 2003 for PC. There are slight variations with keystrokes and mouse clicks for other versions and for Mac.)

- Formatting the page
- Sorting
- Filtering
- Freezing panes
- Hiding columns
- Page preview
- Setup

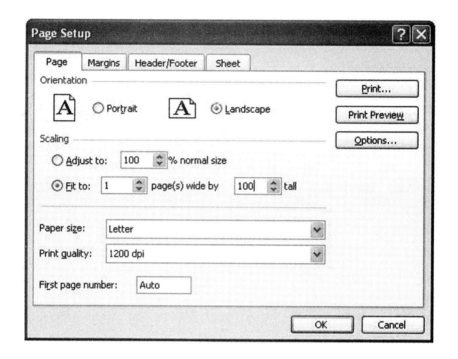

- Layout
- Header/footer
- Gridlines

FORMATTING THE PAGE

Once you've got your wine collection put away the way you want it, it's time to plug in the laptop. You'll probably need an extension cord. Get Excel up and running. Open a fresh page and save it as Wine_Cellar.xls. Along the top row you need to enter the following headers: Type, Producer, Designation,* Designation 2, Vintage, Quantity, Column, Row, and Size.

....

* I use two designations, but you may find it simpler to use one and combine the information from both fields. Two examples: Bruno Giacosa (Designation) Barolo (Designation 2) Le Rocche; and Guigal (Designation) Cote Rotie, (Designation 2) La Turque.

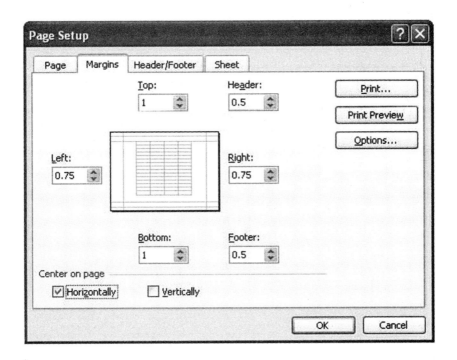

You're going to have to do a few things to make this look better. Under <u>F</u>ile, select Page Setup.

1. Under the <u>Page</u> tab, select Landscape. This will turn the page on its side. Below that, where it says <u>Fit To</u>, select one page wide by ninety-nine pages tall (any number larger than the actual number of pages will suffice).

2. Under the <u>Margins</u> tab, center the page <u>horizontally</u>.

3. Under the <u>Header/Footer</u> tab, select <u>Custom Header</u>. In the center section, type in the words "The Jones Cellar." You may want to put this in a different <u>font</u>, or a different <u>font size</u>. (I like twenty-two point type.) You may also want to put a custom footer at the bottom of the page. I always do, but you may not need the words "Carte du Vin" on your inventory.

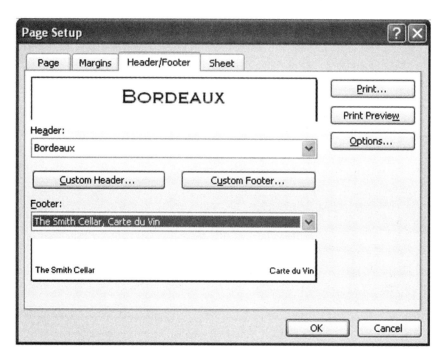

4. A <u>Custom Footer</u> can be useful for noting document information, such as the page number, file name, etc.

5. Under <u>Sheet</u>, you're going to select <u>Gridlines</u>.

6. You're also going to move the cursor to the empty box next to <u>Rows To Repeat At Top</u>. Then you're going to move the cursor to the top line, the one with all the header titles, Row 1, and click on it. This will tell the empty box that you want this line to show up on every page of your inventory. If you see something that says $1:$1, click on <u>OK</u>, and it will be done. (Note: The shortcut to Print Preview is the icon that looks like a sheet of paper with a little magnifying glass and is usually next to the Printer icon on the toolbar at the top of the screen. For reasons I don't fully understand, the Rows to Repeat at Top function is not available when you use the Print Preview icon, only when you go through File and Page Setup from the toolbar. Now you know.)

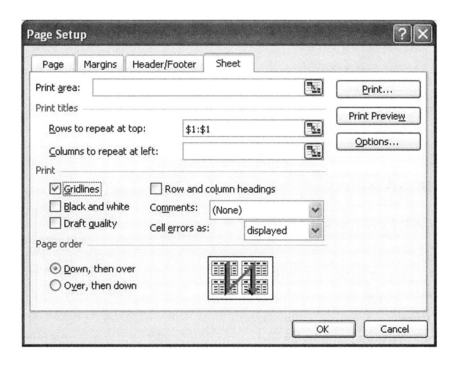

7. You should still be in Print Preview, so you'll see how the sheet looks. You will want to move the margins to make the columns for Producer, Designation 1 and Designation 2 wider. Select <u>Margins</u> and manually move the margins by clicking-and-dragging at the lines between 'A,' 'B,' and 'C.'

8. Before you get too carried away, you'll want to Freeze the top line so that it appears at the top of the page and stays in place no matter how much information you input. Place the cursor in square A2, then select <u>Window</u> from the Task bar. Select <u>Freeze Panes</u> from the drop-down menu. (Repeat the process to <u>Unfreeze Panes</u>.)

I should note that there are built-in redundancies for all the computer moves that allow you to stay on the keyboard, as opposed to using the mouse. Here's an example: To put <u>Gridlines</u> on, as above, can be accomplished from the page by doing the following:

1. Alt + F = <u>F</u>ile
2. V = Print Pre<u>v</u>iew
3. Alt + S = <u>S</u>etup
4. Shift + Right Arrow = tab over to the <u>Sheet</u> tab
5. Alt + G = <u>G</u>ridlines
6. Enter = OK

I use a combination of mouse clicks and keystrokes. I'll try to indicate some more as we go along.

CAPTURING THE DATA

Okay, so now you've got your sheet set up in such a way that you are prepared to enter the data. You've got a guy. You've moved 'em out and put 'em back the way you want them. Now you're ready, "Finally," I can hear you saying, to capture the data. You and the guy are going to split up the work, divide and conquer. Beginning in Column 1, Row A, one of you starts calling out the wines in order while the other enters the information into the spreadsheet. The Type of wine and Producer are self-explanatory. The first Designation will denote different things, depending on the wine's type. In Bordeaux, it will be the Appellation. In California, it is the Vineyard. In Italy and Rhone, the type of wine.

I can't emphasize this enough: the most important thing in this phase of the inventory is consistency. Whichever way you begin to go, stick with it.

You should have put the wine away by region, so that all the Bordeaux are in one area, Rhones are in another, etc. For the moment, let's assume that you know Margaux is from Bordeaux. Whoever is calling out the bottles should do it in the prescribed order: Producer, then Designation (in some cases you may already know this information, for instance, *Latour is in Pauillac*) then vintage. Then comes the location information: Column number and

Type	Producer	Designation	Designation 2	Vintage	Quantity	Column	Row	Size
CAB	Louis Martini	Special Selection		1985	1	218	S	
CAB	Martin Ray	Diamond Mountain		1997	1	69	Q	
CAB	Martin Ray	Synthesis		1997	1	297	O	
CAB	Maya	Dalla Valle		1988	1	69	T	
CAB	Mayacamas	Napa Valley		1985	2	222	D-E	
CAB	Mayacamas	Napa Valley		1971	10	63	M-V	
CAB	Mayacamas	Napa Valley		1974	6	63	G-L	
CAB	Mondavi	Napa Valley		1971	1	217	S	375
CAB	Mondavi	Napa Valley		1974	13	66	I-V	
CAB	Mondavi	Reserve		1985	1	82	L	M
CAB	Mondavi	Reserve		1994	1	83	F	M
CAB	Mondavi	Reserve		1974	1	66	K	
CAB	Mondavi	Reserve		1985	6	66	C-H	
CAB	Mondavi	Reserve		1994	2	66	A-B	
CAB	Mondavi	Reserve		1997	5	299	O-S	
CAB	Monterrey Peninsula	Monterrey		1975	12	223	D-O	
CAB	Montrose	St Estephe		1990	2	83	I-J	M
CAB	Mount Eden	Saratoga		1973	3	218	D-F	
CAB	Optima	Alexander Valley		1990	1	222	O	
CAB	Pas de Deux	Artist Series		1997	6	56	M-O	
CAB	Plumpjack	Oakville		1997	4	64	A-D	
CAB	Ridge	York Creek		1984	2	59	J-K	
CAB	Rosenthal	Newton Canyon		1994	1	79	M	M
CAB	Rubissow sargent	Mt. Veeder		1988	1	220	L	
CAB	S. Anderson	Stag's Leap District		1997	6	298	O-T	
CAB	Shafer	Hillside Select		1997	6	84	B-G	
CAB	Shafer	Napa Valley		1978	6	225	Q-V	
CAB	Showket	Oakville		2000	1	67	A	
CAB	Silverado	Limited Reserve		1997	5	69	L-P	
CAB	Sonoma Vineyards	Alexander		1974	4	219	K-N	
CAB	Spring Mountain	Reserve		1997	4	293	M-R	
CAB	St. Clement	Napa Valley		1994	1	78	N	M
CAB	St. Clement	Napa Valley		1997	5	299	J-N	
CAB	Staglin Family	Rutherford		1994	1	81	C	M
CAB	Staglin Family	Rutherford		1997	6	300	R-W	
CAB	Stag's Leap Cellars	Cask 23		1977	2	62	I-J	
CAB	Stag's Leap Cellars	Cask 23		1985	1	62	K	
CAB	Stag's Leap Cellars	Cask 23		1997	3	62	L-N	

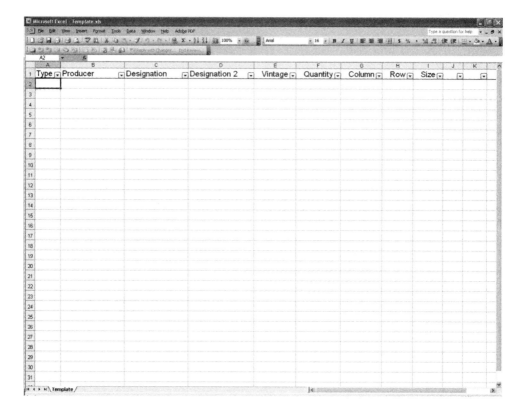

Row letters. If there are more than two bottles of a certain title, they should be directly next to their kinsmen.

A typical dialogue goes like this: "I have Jayer Vosne Romanee Cros Parantoux '89 six times in 1, A–F."

This is the point where I say: "'89?"

And my guy, Drew, says, "Roger that!"

This is a lot of information to be passing back and forth, and it will serve you well to confirm the message or any parts of it that you're not absolutely certain of.

With Bordeaux and California wines, you should be able to make do with one Designation. With Burgundy, Rhone and Italian wine, however, there will generally be two Designations. It's important to keep the information as standardized as you can. I put the type of wine (e.g., Chateauneuf-du-Pape) in the Designation 1 column, and any additional qualifier (e.g., Cuvee Laurence, Reserve, or La Chapelle) in Designation 2.

Note: Save your information often. The process above takes time, and bad things happen with computers, especially laptops, where a field can get highlighted and accidentally deleted. It's possible to do something that rearranges the data in a way you did not intend, and you then have to go back and fix it. Having already saved your master file as Wine_Cellar.xls, you may want to save different versions as you go along, so that you have Wine_Cellar1.0.xls, Wine_Cellar1.1.xls, and so on, every hour or so. You can move the old versions into an Archives file, but it means that you'll never be more than an hour away from where the "bad thing" happened.

Make copies of your information. I keep a copy on disc and on a USB memory key, and I transfer the information to my desktop. The only problem with having been so thorough with saving the data is that you've now got four copies. Make sure you know which one is the Master copy if you're going to make changes. (More on this later, in Maintenance).

SEARCHING

When you're putting everything away, inevitably you're going to come across the wine you put "over there" that matches up with something you've already entered. There are several ways to find the others, including Sorting and by using Filters, as described below. The quickest way to jump around directly to something is by performing a Search.

1. Hit Ctrl + F
2. Enter what you're looking for in the window.
3. Click on Find Next until you get to what you're looking for.

FILTERS

Filters are also a Data function that allows you to screen out only the information you need to see from an entire list.

Filters are going to be very helpful to you when you're inputting data and you have a sneaking suspicion that you've already seen a certain title and want to match up a stray bottle with its kinsmen.

- To turn Filters on, highlight the Header Row by clicking on number one on the far left of the screen.
- When the row is highlighted, select Data from the Task Bar.
- Select Filters from the drop-down menu.
- Then select Auto-Filter. (The built-in redundancy allows you to achieve the same results by hitting Alt + D, then F, then Enter (or F), when Auto Filter is highlighted.)

Filters are also helpful when you want see all the wines you have in a certain year (a "horizontal" as opposed to a "vertical," which is the same wine from different years). Click on the drop-down menu in the "Vintage" column. You should see a listing of every year you've entered. Scroll down and select a year. All the wines from that year will be filtered out. To reset the list, click on the drop-down menu again, scroll up to the top and select "All" at the top of the menu.

Word of caution: you can delete the data in a column when the Filters are on, and you can hide a column when the Filters are on, but you cannot delete a column or move a column when the Filters are on. If you need to move or delete a column, turn the Filters off, make the adjustment, then turn the Filters back on.

SORTING

Sorting is a Data function that allows you to prioritize the data you've collected by any of the column headings. I usually order my

information by (1) Type or Region, (2) Producer, (3) Vintage, but I have a client who places Producer first. It's up to you.

1. From the taskbar at the top of the screen, select Data.
2. Click on Sort from the drop down menu.
3. The pop-up screen offers you three windows that allow you to select the order in which you want the data sorted. For example, if you want to get everything together by Type in alphabetical order, so that the Bordeaux are grouped together, followed by Burgundy, Cabernet, etc., you would:
4. Make sure that Data Range "Header Row" is selected in the line below the three windows. This should highlight everything in your data fields except the Header Row.*
5. Enter Type (you can scroll down from a menu) in the first window and select Ascending order.

....
* *If you don't do this, you will be including the Header Row in the field to be sorted, and you'll find this row, which begins with Type, sandwiched alphabetically between Syrah and Zinfandel.*

6. Enter Producer in the next window and select Ascending order (A–Z).

7. Enter Vintage in the last window, and select Ascending order (oldest to youngest).

8. Click on OK.

(The built-in redundancy here allows you to achieve the same results by hitting Alt + D, then hitting S).

Now you may want to further sort the individual Types of wine. In Rhone, the same producer (Guigal) produces four separate Cote-Roties listed in the Designation 2 column (La Landonne, La Mouline, and La Turque, plus a "generic" one). The Sort function described above would have all the Cote-Roties arranged by vintage, not by Designation 2.

1. From the Filters drop-down menu at the top of the Type column, select Rhone (or whichever Type you want to re-sort). This will show only the Rhone wines.

2. Choose Sort from the Data menu on the task bar, as above.

3. Again, making sure that your list has a Header row.

4. Enter Producer in the first window (you can scroll down from the choices on the Header row).

5. Enter Designation in the second window.

6. Enter Designation 2 in the third window.

Because the list is already pre-sorted by vintage, this should give you all of the La Landonnes, etc., together in ascending vintage order. I also use this function to help make sense of Burgundy and Italians wines. In Burgundy, the problem is that a single Producer might make several different wines.

In Italy, use the Designation field to show the type of wine (Italy is the Type), so an Italian entry might read: (Type) Italy; (Producer) Giacosa, Bruno; (Designation) Barolo; (Designation 2) Riserva; (Vintage) 1997. Eventually, because the wines are listed in

Alphabetical order by producer, Italy becomes a bit of a jumble of Barolos, Barbarescos, Brunellos, Chiantis, and what I group together as "Red Table Wines," a group which includes Super-Tuscans, Merlot and Cabernet-based wines, and anything else that seems to defy description beyond Vino da Tavola. If you've only got one page of Italian wines (what I think of as "a good start"), it might be easier to see it listed by producer. As the collection grows to two or more pages, you may want to make better sense of this by re-sorting by these types of wine Designation.

1. From the Filters drop-down menu, select Italy (It may be easier to do this by cutting-and-pasting all the Italian wines to another worksheet. Name this sheet Italian).
2. Select Sort from the Data menu on the taskbar.
3. Making sure your list has a Header Row, as above.
4. Enter Designation in the top window.
5. Enter Producer in the second window.
6. Enter Designation 2 in the bottom window.

This will group all of the Barolos, etc., together, alphabetically by producer. If there are differences within a single Producer's offerings; they will be sorted alphabetically under Designation 2; and because you've previously sorted this information by vintage, everything should be in order from oldest to youngest. So far, so good.

HIDING COLUMNS

Now I start to make it more legible. The amount of information on a sheet can shrink the type, so I try to remove any extraneous columns wherever possible.

At the top of each of the Designation groups (Barolo, Barbaresco, etc.), insert a Row.

1. Right-click on the top row, the first entry of a new group. (Note: The first grouping, in this case Barolo, is where you'll want to insert this row above the Header Row, From the menu, select Insert. A blank Row will appear.

2. Move into the blank field in the Producer column, so that it is rimmed in black.

3. From the toolbar at the top of the screen, change the Font size from ten to eighteen.

4. Enter the name of the type of wine from the Designation column, e.g., Barolo.

5. Repeat with each type of wine. (While I don't want to over-complicate an already complicated scenario, I've found it's simpler—it saves a couple of keystrokes, and they do add up—to make all the Inserts at once, then copy the eighteen point title into the appointed fields, and re-type over them).

When you have put all the different types together, Right-Click on the top of the Designation column and choose Hide. (You'll also want to hide the Type column, as they will all be Italy.)

1. Go in to Print Preview.
2. Under Setup, select Header/Footer.
3. Select Custom Header.
4. Enter the word Italy (or Italian Wines) in the center field.
5. Highlight "Italy" and change the font size to twenty-two. (You may also change the font itself, if you'd prefer).
6. When you're satisfied with your handiwork, select OK and OK again.
7. You may want to adjust the margins a bit (Click and drag from the top of each column).

If you've done this on the Master file, you will have to go back through and delete these rows after you've printed them out.

Note: Make sure that under File/Page Setup/Sheet, you've selected to repeat the Header Row at the top.

Type	Producer	Designation	Designation 2	Vintage	Quant	Column	Row	Size
BOR	Durfort Vivens			1966	8	286	A-H	
BOR	Durfort Vivens			1970	3	288	R-T	
BOR	Fetit Clinet	Pomerol		1970	1	81	D	M
BOR	Feytit Clinet	Pomerol		1970	1	284	H	
BOR	Feytit Clinet	Pomerol		1970	1	M2	I	M
BOR	Figeac	St. Emilion		2000	3	276	A-C	
BOR	Figeac	St. Emilion		1966	1	45	C	
BOR	Giscours	Margaux		1928	1	46	K	
BOR	Giscours	Margaux		1966	1	285	H	
BOR	Giscours	Margaux		1970	2	285	F-G	
BOR	Grand Corbin Despagne	St. Emilion		1964	1	286	V	
BOR	Grand Puy Lacoste	Pauillac		1964	1	22	F	
BOR	Grand Puy Lacoste	Pauillac		1966	3	285	C-E	
BOR	Grand Puy Lacoste	Pauillac		1982	4	37	E-H	
BOR	Grand Puy Lacoste	Pauillac		2000	6	276	G-I	
BOR	Gruaud Larose	St. Julien		1953	2	45	K-L	
BOR	Gruaud Larose	St. Julien		1985	4	37	A-D	
BOR	Gruaud Larose	St. Julien		2000	6	275	G-I	
BOR	Gruaud Larose	St. Julien		1986	17	50	M-U	
BOR	Haut Batailley			1982	5	51	O-Q	
BOR	Haut Brion	Graves		2000	3	275	A-C	
BOR	Haut Brion	Graves		1918	1	29	K	
BOR	Haut Brion	Graves		1945	1	29	J	
BOR	Haut Brion	Graves		1953	2	29	L-M	
BOR	Haut Brion	Graves		1956	1	29	I	
BOR	Haut Brion	Graves		1959	1	30	K	
BOR	Haut Brion	Graves		1966	8	29	N-U	
BOR	Haut Brion	Graves		1967	1	29	H	
BOR	Haut Brion	Graves		1970	5	30	O-S	
BOR	Haut Brion	Graves		1982	3	30	L-N	
BOR	Haut Brion	Graves		1989	2	29	F-G	
BOR	Haut Brion	Graves		1989	1	Display	Rack	6L
BOR	Haut Brion	Graves		1990	7	30	D-J	
BOR	Haut Brion	Graves		2000	2	Display	Rack	M
BOR	La Conseillante	Pomerol		1979	1	20	B	
BOR	La Conseillante	Pomerol		2000	3	278	G-I	
BOR	La Fleur de Gay	Pomerol		1989	2	21	N-O	
BOR	La Gaffeliere	St. Emilion		1982	1	22	E	

PRINTING FROM THE MASTER FILE

There are two ways to Print the list. You can simply run a copy of the master file, but there are things you can do to "prettify" it.

1. Using the Filters, select Bordeaux in Column A. As described above, this will leave only those wines that read "Bordeaux" in Column A.
2. Now hide Column A.
3. Hide Column D (Designation 2) because there's nothing in there.
4. Go into Print Preview and select Setup.
5. Select the Custom Header and Footer, then click on Custom Header.
6. Type "Bordeaux" as your custom header.
7. Take a long look at it before hitting the Print button.

When you're done with Bordeaux, move on to the next category. You'll have to resurrect Column A by clicking and dragging (or double-clicking) on the place where Column A ought to be.

As they say on the back of the shampoo bottle, rinse and repeat. Make sure you enter a new Header in each time, and make sure you either Hide or Unhide Column D, depending on whether or not there is information in there you want to see (e.g. Burgundy, Italy, Rhone).

PRINTING TO INDIVIDUAL SHEETS
SCORES & HOLD 'TIL & DRINK BY DATES

Now you've got your inventory lined up in apple-pie order, the list is sorted, and it is gorgeous. You are the envy of all your friends. People are lining up to have wild sex with you. Now let's fill it out.

1. Column J: Robert Parker or RP (for Robert Parker)
2. Column K: *Wine Spectator* or WS (for *Wine Spectator*)

3. Column L: Hold 'Til
4. Column M: Drink By
5. Column N: Price

I cannot suggest strongly enough getting some version of Parker. There is the online version (*www.erobertparker.com*) available for ninety-nine dollars a year; the software version is about the same price, and comes with annual updates (damn lot of good that'll do you when you're trying to validate the latest releases) and the new Parker-in-your-Palm version for your PDA. Any and all of these have the Great One's ratings, plus suggested Hold 'Til/Drink By dates.

The WineSpectator.com site also has scores and sometimes, but less often, the suggested Hold 'Til and Drink By dates. Their dates tend to suggest you drink the wines younger. Their prices are much more reliable, however, than are Parker's, who seems to have bought just about everything on release, a million years ago when the world was young. Both sites have extensive listings and are well worth the price of admission.

PRICES

I take my prices from a variety of sources. The best place to establish the value of a bottle of wine is *www.winesearcher.com*. Their amazingly quick search engine scours the sites of 1,827 stores from around the world, which stock a combined total of nearly one million wines. The service is free, but I highly recommend their "professional" version, with a nominal membership fee of fifteen dollars per year. It gives you more of the same, but you could easily save the subscription fee with your first purchase. (I use it so often that it's my "home page.") The best place to determine the price of a bottle of wine at auction online is a subscription site *www.winemarketjournal.com*.

The other great place to find auction prices is: Vinfolio's Price file (www.vinfolio.com). This amazing reference book lists every

	Type	Producer	Designation	Vintage	Quantity	Column	Row	Size	RP	WS	Hold Ti	Drink B	Price
200	BOR	Le Pin	Pomerol	1998	2	43	I		93-96	95-99	2003	2018	1008
201	BOR	L'Eglise Clinet	Pomerol	1921	1	67	G	M	100	-	-	-	12540
202	BOR	L'Eglise Clinet	Pomerol	1947	1	66	F	M	100	-	-	-	13500
203	BOR	L'Eglise Clinet	Pomerol	1985	2	45	G		95	94	2001	2020	220
204	BOR	L'Eglise Clinet	Pomerol	1990	2	45	G		92	94	1999	2017	230
205	BOR	L'Eglise Clinet	Pomerol	1998	12	33	D-E		94	96	2008	2035	239
206	BOR	Leoville Las Cases	Pauillac	2000	12	34	B-G		99	100	2010	2035	145
207	BOR	Leoville Las Cases	St Julien	1978	3	37	B-C		90	94	1995	2015	113
208	BOR	Leoville Las Cases	St Julien	1983	7	37	G-J		91	87	1995	2010	95
209	BOR	Leoville Las Cases	St Julien	1985	5	37	D-F		93	94	1997	2015	139
210	BOR	Leoville Las Cases	St Julien	1990	3	39	I-J		96	93	2002	2027	182
211	BOR	Leoville Las Cases	St Julien	1995	5	39	F-H		95	95	2005	2025	129
212	BOR	L'Evangile	Pomerol	1995	6	44	R-T		92+	94	2005	2020	132
213	BOR	L'Evangile	Pomerol	1998	12	30	W-R		92	95-99	2003	2020	213
214	BOR	Lynch Bages	Pauillac	1961	2	35	B-C		95	88	2000	2010	700
215	BOR	Lynch Bages	Pauillac	1982	3	37	M-N		94	96	2000	2015	220
216	BOR	Lynch Bages	Pauillac	1985	2	37	O-P		92	97	2000	2010	162
217	BOR	Lynch Bages	Pauillac	1986	3	37	R-S		92	94	2003	2020	134
218	BOR	Lynch Bages	Pauillac	1988	3	37	T-U		92	97	2000	2012	118
219	BOR	Lynch Bages	Pauillac	1989	5	36	B-D		95	98	2004	2030	174
220	BOR	Lynch Bages	Pauillac	1990	3	37	V-W		94	94	2000	2020	165
221	BOR	Lynch Bages	Pauillac	1995	9	36	R-W		91	94	2005	2020	66
222	BOR	Lynch Bages	Pauillac	2000	11	36	E-J		95	96	2008	2025	140
223	BOR	Margaux	Margaux	1900	2	39	K		100	93	1994	2030	4200
224	BOR	Margaux	Margaux	1928	1	39	K		98	84	1994	2028	1695
225	BOR	Margaux	Margaux	1953	1	71	K	M	98	84	-	-	995
226	BOR	Margaux	Margaux	1961	1	40	K		93	92	1991	2001	924
227	BOR	Margaux	Margaux	1982	2	39	L		94	95	2005	2035	472
228	BOR	Margaux	Margaux	1983	6	39	M-O		96	98	2002	2030	299
229	BOR	Margaux	Margaux	1985	3	39	P-Q		94	95	1997	2010	311
230	BOR	Margaux	Margaux	1986	6	39	R-U		96	98	2000	2050	275
231	BOR	Margaux	Margaux	1995	3	40	L-M		95	100	2005	2040	262
232	BOR	Margaux	Margaux	2000	12	C	15		99	95-100	2010	2050	316
233	BOR	Monbousquet	St. Emilion	2000	6	46	P-R		96	85-89	2006	2020	135
234	BOR	Mouton Rothschild	Pauillac	1945	1	75	M	M	100	94	1997	2047	12750
235	BOR	Mouton Rothschild	Pauillac	1955	3	35	L-M		97	95	1994	2024	495
236	BOR	Mouton Rothschild	Pauillac	1959	2	35	K		100	99	1997	2027	1200
237	BOR	Mouton Rothschild	Pauillac	1959	1	74	L	M	100	99	1997	2027	2850
238	BOR	Mouton Rothschild	Pauillac	1959	1	79	O	M	100	99	1997	2027	2850

auction price paid for a bottle of wine over the past several years. It may be more information than you need to know, but it establishes a range of high and low estimates for the most collectible wines in the world.

The process of laying in the scores is quite tedious and, if you have a lot of wine, it's going to take a little time. I hate this work, and I've recently hired research assistants to do it for me. I've also put together a database of my own that lists every bottle I've run across during my career, over twelve thousand titles currently. (There have literally been millions of wines produced over the years, but the ones that are collected show up fairly consistently from one cellar to the next.)

APPRAISAL VALUE

Let's stipulate that at this point you have entered all the prices, using all the tools listed above. Now it's time to enter a formula to get a grand total. If you've done this as I've suggested, the Quantity is in Column F, and the Price is in Column N. (If you've entered other information that changes where Quantity & Price are, adjust the following equation accordingly.)

1. In Column O, Row 2, you are going to enter a formula that reads as follows: =f2*n2, then hit Enter. This should give you the number of bottles (from F) times the price per bottle (from N). So far, so good. Now let's expand that to the entire list.

2. Highlight O2. Now click and drag it down the length of Column O to the very last entry. This will apply the same formula to each row.

3. Now go to the bottom of Column O, to the blank space at the bottom of the list of totals. Hit the Σ key on the toolbar at the top of the screen. This totals the column.

There is, as ever, a shortcut to this.

1. Click on O2
2. Ctrl + C
3. Shift + Left Arrow ?
4. Move the mouse to the bottom of cell N2 and double-click, highlighting Columns N and O.
5. Shift + Right Arrow ?
6. Ctrl +V
7. Move the mouse to the empty space at the bottom of column O.
8. Double-Click on Σ from the tool bar at top.

Most of the software programs on the market allow you to enter the purchase price or the current value or both. If you have a list of what you've bought and when, it's best to wait until the end and enter them once you've got the inventory together.

Putting It Online

There are a couple of ways of getting your cellar online. The simplest is a new Web site designed by a Microsoft employee, Eric LeVine (I'm not so sure that's his real name): *www.cellartracker.com.* He has created a virtual community of wine collectors, all eager to share tasting notes. The site is a little clunky, but it does the job better than most people could do themselves.

I have a hidden page on my Web site for my clients where they can enter a user name and a password to see their collections on-line. Once I've got the pages formatted for printing, I put them all into a .pdf file. You'll need to get a .pdf file maker. Adobe is the standard, but their product is very expensive (one hundred and fifty to three hundred dollars), and if you don't use the other features it offers, it's not a good investment. There are plenty of others available for downloading for fifteen to fifty dollars, or shareware you can try for free. Go to Cnet.com or Google and take a look around. I use one from *www.docudesk.com*.

When you've got the .pdf file maker program loaded onto your computer, print the files you want to post online. When the printer folder comes up, choose the .pdf file maker from the list of printers. It will only take a second to convert. Name the file, e.g., Bordeaux.pdf.

I have a Web site with an automated loading mechanism, but not everyone has their own Web site, so go to *www.Blogger.com* and get an account. It's free and easy to do. (Even I managed to get through the registration process without having to call in an expert.)

1. Once inside your account, choose Create New Post.
2. Select Upload File at the top of the window.
3. Browse through your documents and select the Bordeaux.pdf file.
4. Select Upload File at the lower right.
5. You'll get an http file name.
6. Preview your post, then select Publish Your Post.
7. Voila! You're on the air!

Putting It on Your Handheld

As a bells-and-whistles service, I started putting the inventories on a PDA, Palm Pilot, Handheld—call it what you will. The Palm and Microsoft-based units have some kind of document converter that will allow you to transfer an Excel spreadsheet. (My Sony Clie has a utility called "Documents To Go" by a company called Dataviz. You can download the program from *www.Dataviz.com* if your unit doesn't come with it.)

This particular feature actually has some practical applications. I brought my Clie with me to a pre-auction tasting at Christie's, where I was planning to meet some of their specialists for the first time and explain my business to them. I opened up the Burgundy page of a fantastic collection. As I was scrolling down, I saw that they were offering a vintage of Comte de Vogue Musigny that would fit into this guy's vertical like a piece of a jigsaw puzzle. I called the guy, we entered a bid, and he bought the bottle in the auction.

It's good to have access to your holdings when you're traveling, at restaurants, etc. People love to see that the bottle they bought for thirty-five dollars is now selling at a restaurant for three hundred and fifty dollars.

The biggest problem with having your inventory on a handheld is that the screen is really small and the page is really wide. In preparation, you may want to lose a little information, especially the location of each bottle. Do you really need to know where it is, or just that you've got it? I shrink all the columns down to the bare essentials. Instead of the word "Quantity," I put the ## sign, or just "Q." Instead of "Vintage," I use "Yr" or "V", and I get rid of all the 19s and 20s in the Vintage column. (Assuming you don't have a lot of wines from 1900–1905, this shouldn't present much of a conflict.) Same thing in the Hold 'Til and Drink By Columns. Price becomes $$$.

1. Open the Documents-to-Go from the icon on the desktop, or in your program files. (This is a good one to keep on the desktop.)
2. Choose Add Item
3. Scan through your files until you find the one you want, then click on it.
4. Repeat as necessary.

5. When you're done adding the files you want, close out of the Documents-To-Go window.
6. <u>Synch</u> up your PDA as you normally would. This will take a little longer than usual.

Neck Tags

I hate neck tags, wait, let me think about it. No, I hate them. They look awful and defeat the purpose of my inventory system or any inventory program. Further, if you put them on every bottle it makes things harder to find and more confusing, thus defeating their purpose. The room looks like an eye chart.

Even so, in some cellars I think neck tags can be useful. In one cellar, I used them to distinguish the best bottles from the riff-raff. Another guy wanted a color-coded (red-yellow-green) system that told him when to open each bottle. Green means Go!

If you must use neck tags, type the labels.

Bar Coding

Clients occasionally ask me for a bar coding system. I've seen them, I know how to set one up, and I recommend against it. The system is quite expensive; it requires a dedicated computer, new hardware, new software, and more new junk to learn. It's subject to breakdowns (don't call me when it does) and makes the job of reorganizing a cellar much more difficult.

Imagine if you will, a grid of twenty columns and twenty rows, filled with wine bottles. Let us assume (I hate to, but we really must) that some of it was bought in different quantities of one, two, three, four, six or twelve. Let's further assume that all the like wines are kept together, so that a case of something runs down a column in rows A-L. (Are you with me, so far?) Let's further assume that when you remove bottles from this grid—one Meursault from here, one Shiraz from there—your grid will start to look like a moth-eaten sweater. Okay, now you've gone through twelve bottles and a case of wine shows up at your door. Where you gonna put 'em, slugger? Huh?

In Carte du Vin's world, you push a little here, pull a little there, and pretty soon you've created space for a dozen like bottles. In Bar Code world, you can put the case away in the available holes, all over the place, but where's the beauty in that? It has all the symmetry of a melanoma. Besides which, I think the reports this thing prints out are horrible. I wouldn't put my name on them.

I know one wine collector who installed a bar code system and is happy with it. He is the very well-to-do owner of a top Napa winery who has someone on staff to take care of his cellar for him. He is the first to admit that he doesn't have a clue as to how the bar code system actually functions, all he knows is that is suits him and it works great.

There are a couple of commercially available bar-coding systems. eSommelier (*www.esommelier.net*) has a web-enabled touch-screen kiosk that can interface with home A/V command systems like Creston so you can check out your stash from keypad screens around the house. The system takes some getting used to but does a great job tracking your holdings. At $5,000–$10,000, it ought to.

Other nifty gadgets include the Intelliscanner (*www.intellisw .com*) with Blue Tooth technology, that like eSommelier, reads barcodes on bottles. Unfortunately, most "collectble" wines don't have bar codes and need to have them applied with a separate sticker.

You can also find bar code scanners and printers that can be adapted for wine cellar inventory at *www.zebra.com*.

One thing to keep in mind with any of these electronic bells and whistles is that somebody has to capture the data and enter it into the correct fields. Hardware, like software, doesn't type.

Radio-wave technology is just coming into the market, it is the equivalent of a GPS (Global Positioning System) and is used to track each bottle's whereabouts. A small tag is placed on the bottle. If it moves out of range, it gets deducted from inventory. If it comes back to the cellar, it automatically updates the inventory. What will they think of next?

Maintenance

If setting up a cellar for the first time is akin to landscape architecture, then my maintenance program is like having a gardener come in to weed out and rake the leaves.

Some of my clients just need to get the inventory and then they want to take care of it themselves from there. They have the organizational sensibility, the computer skills, and the obsessive personality to keep it up to date.

Most, however, are happy to have me come back to keep things in apple-pie order for them. I think that most of these guys have housekeepers, and gardeners, and all kinds of people who take care of things for them that they'd rather not spend their free time doing. They could grow their own vegetables, but they don't. They don't fix their cars either.

Once you've got a master inventory list, you need to keep track of what goes out and what comes in, and where you put the new bottles. I created an *In and Out* cellar inventory tracking sheet for a client in Las Vegas who doesn't have a computer. The header row includes In/Out, Wine, Vintage, Quantity, Location and Price Paid. I made a blank sheet of this and he fills it in and faxes it to me

to update every so often. (A copy is available at *www.thebestcellar
.com/templates*.)

Accept that your inventory is always going to be off by a little bit. There's almost no getting around it. I set up my clients with a book, a CD-RW with a spreadsheet file for their computer, a page on my Web site, and even on their handheld PDA (Palm Pilot). If they take one bottle out, it means that the inventory is wrong in four different places. While I strive to be 100 percent accurate, I'm pretty happy when it's 99 percent of the way there. (For the record—Carte du Vin doesn't make "mistakes," but there are occasionally "discrepancies.") Depending on the size of the collection, most people who use an *In and Out* inventory-tracking sheet find it's sufficient to update their inventory every three to six months.

When you get new wine, you're eventually going to have to put it away (unless you call me, but even then *someone* is going to have to put it away). When preparing the initial inventory, I try to leave some space for new acquisitions, but that too will fill up, and space is at a premium. You're going to have to pull and push a bit to make room, and you've got to keep track of those changes on your Master file as you go along. Again, it's easier to work with a guy calling out the changes. Once you've gotten started and gotten used to manipulating the data in certain ways, it will be a breeze.

Keep archives of your old files and back-up your system. You move a lot of data around on these spreadsheets, and you want to really don't want to lose it all because of one errant keystroke. Save a disc copy every once in a while or keep a dupe on another computer.

5

Collectors

Wine collectors are a breed apart; they build up their cellars with the notion of tearing it down as they go.

What separates them is an attitude exemplified by how you answer this word problem: If you have 1,000 bottles at an average value of $100 and take two out to drink, are you richer or poorer?

The stamp collector would see an asset diminished by $200, but the wine collector would say he's richer for the experience.

I've met many different types of collectors since I started this business, and they are an eclectic, eccentric bunch. People who spend large amounts of money collecting perishable things have to be a little nuts. Every collector is a combination of these twelve basic characteristics.

The Wannabe

I had a client who knew absolutely nothing about wine—except that he liked it. He said, "Jeff, I've got a big job with a lot of responsibility. I've got two little children. I've got a wife who's a pain in the ass. And I've got golf game that's in serious trouble. I don't have any time left to read the *Wine Spectator*. That's why I need you."

I told the Wannabe that we should sit down and open up some wine to try to determine where his palate was, what kind of wines he liked, and we'd go from there. "I know what kind of wine I like."

"Really? What kind?"

"I like French wine."

Well, you can imagine the sense of relief I felt. That certainly narrowed down the search. That simplified *everything*. I'd just run out to the French Wine Shop and ask them for about two hundred cases of French Wine, and he'd be all set.

We did, in fact, buy quite a bit of wine together, French and otherwise, and we've become quite good friends over time. I suggested that he should have a dinner party for some friends where I'd cook and we could open up some of these bottles—a sort of christening party for the cellar. For the main course we served Mouton '82 out of individual crystal decanters. I told him, "When you open this stuff in your beautiful home, surrounded by friends who appreciate it, you're sitting on top of the world."

He still doesn't know anything about wine, but he's knows that much.

Small Time

Small Time is an accident that has already happened. He's fallen and he can't get up. His collection of a couple hundred bottles seems to have happened by mistake. As the old saw goes, "If you don't know where you're going, any road will get you there." He doesn't know what he has, or even what he likes. What he does know is that there is some elusive wine that's better than what he's got, but he's not sure how to take the first steps toward fixing the problem. As they say on the *X-Files*, "The answer is out there."

Small Time is the embodiment of buyer's remorse. He occasionally steps up to the plate and buys a case of something, only to recognize immediately that he's made a mistake. When he's in the unfortunate position of having to open a bottle for someone he thinks is knowledgeable, he asks them, "How do you think this is?"

Small Time's taste is going to change.

The Farmer

My client, Dr. Farmer, wants to try everything under the sun and winds up with a "bottle farm"—one of each type of wine, one from each producer. He has almost exactly one thousand bottles in his collection on seven hundred and fifty line-listings, an average of about 1.3 bottles per title. He buys mixed cases. Not mixed cases like six plus six or four and four and four. No. He buys twelve unique bottles in each case. So I asked him, "What's up, doc?" (I waited almost my whole life to say that.)

He said that he gets bored.

Bored! I could kill this guy with my bare hands. Whatever happened to the idea that you try one bottle from a case when it's young and coltish, get a sense of it, make a note in your journal, lock it away in your memory? Open another bottle when you suspect, or when Mr. Parker suggests, that it will be ready to drink, yet is still vivacious, jejune. It's a completely different experience. Drink the others in their prime and save a couple to enjoy in their (and maybe your) declining years.

There was a wonderful jazz disc jockey in LA named Chuck Niles. He'd been around since the dawn of recorded sound, with a great basso vibrato voice. He once said that he didn't dig Billie Holiday's later recordings until he, himself, was older. My point is that you're going to want to see these wines through their lives and through your life. A case of wine is not a chicken dinner. It's a twelve-course feast in a box. You can't, or most likely won't, drink them all in one sitting, or one month, or one year, so how, exactly, do you get bored of a great wine? Even a pretty good wine? Heaven forbid he should actually like something and want to try it again. Heaven forbid he should have a party for more than two people. What then? Every time he goes out, it's a crapshoot. He can never say, "I had this wine recently and it was terrific." No, this guy can say something to the point of: "This is the first and last time I'm ever going to try this, so savor the moment, honey."

I hate to admit it, but I'm something of a Farmer, myself. I don't have enough money to buy everything in case lots, or in quantities of fours or sixes, and I see so many appetizing choices at the store that I can't say no to. So many Rhones with scores in the low nineties that you can't choose just one. So many odd-sounding Australian wines at prices that practically scream out, "Try me!"

And there's nothing wrong with doing just that.

The Explorer

The Explorer is interested in the *new* new thing. He is all about moving on. He is like a talent agent who believes you're only as hot as your latest discovery. I told one Explorer about a tasting that included verticals of Phelps Insignia ('77, '85 and '95), Cheval Blanc ('70, '82 and '90), and a horizontal of 1990 Echezeaux from some top producers (Leroy, Jayer and DRC). He called the whole lot of them "Pedestrian." His reasoning, after I got over the shock, was that it didn't take any particular genius to know that these would be good, even great wines. It took some foresight to buy them *then,* but where's the thrill of the hunt in them *now?*

The Explorer is ahead of the curve. He's already been to the restaurant you just heard about. He's on the web, devouring postings. His responses are the subject of table talk at your wine events. He hates when Parker validates his new find, because that signals the beginning of the gold rush. Next year that same wine will come out at twice the price, but he will have moved on again to the next new thing. He disdains the Point Man. When he discovers something new, he acknowledges the lack of a Parker/*Wine Spectator* score as a badge of honor. There's always something new to discover, and the Explorer knows what it is and where to find it.

If the Explorer gives you a tip, act on it quickly.

The Stamp Collector

The Stamp Collector is a guy who collects wine because it is a commodity. A commodity that is valued and traded, the subject of speculation in a constantly fluctuating market. He collects wine because he collects things. He could just as easily be collecting stamps or cars or coins or books or sports memorabilia (he often does collect those things, too). The Stamp Collector has an interest in wine, but it tends to have more to do with the price he paid, or the story that goes with the acquisition of the wine than the experience of drinking it.

The Stamp Collector is obsessed with filling out verticals of different wines. He'll buy off-years that are known to be past their prime just to complete the string, with no intention of ever opening the bottle. It's a stamp.

The Thing to Do

There are more wine collectors now than ever before. Part of that is the increase in the Multi-Millionaires Next Door in this country and around the world. Big new money is not an uncommon thing. There are a lot of guys who hit it out of the park with dot-coms, investment banking, syndication deals or inheritances who bought a house or two, a couple more cars than are strictly necessary, and got into wine because they needed something to do. This collector is keeping up with the other Joneses in a very elite club. It's the Thing to Do. This is especially true of the 'tweeners, the guys who are impossibly wealthy compared to the garden variety rich guy, but can't afford a plane of their own yet (and pretend they don't want one despite their NetJet share).

The Thing to Do may have been into wine before the money came, or he may have gotten into wine because it was the next logical place to burn through a million bucks. He doesn't make mistakes. He started collecting after the IPO money, so he has no reason to make mistakes.

One Thing To Do client explained his newfound interest in wine as we toured his new house. "I've got a home theater system over here, and a wine cellar over there." As far as he was concerned, both rooms needed to be decorated.

The Point Man

I have a funny postcard that I picked up at Sherlock's Wines in Atlanta. A guy tries a wine and tells the salesman it's terrible. When the salesman tells him that the *Wine Snob* magazine gave it a ninety-seven, he says, "I'll take a case!"

The Point Man is the guy who lives and dies by what Mr. Robert

M. Parker Jr. has to say. He doesn't actually read the reviews so much as he reads the little numbers at the bottom of the page. If it got ninety-five points, he wants it. He may not care for Condrieu or Amarone or Pinot Noir, but that's hardly the point. It Got Ninety-Five Points! And that's the point.

While there's something that feels wrong about this approach, I can't quite put my finger on it. If you're at a store and you're choosing between two wines at the same price, but one has a tag reading 88 and the other says 92, why would you buy the former? Aren't Two Thumbs Up better than Two Thumbs Down?

The Point Man lives in a strict meritocracy; he gauges which wine he serves to whom based on how many points he thinks his company deserves.

One Point Man I know is drinking his cellar from bottom to top, so no matter how good the collection gets, you're always guaranteed to get the worst bottle in it. By the time he dies, the cellar will be perfect.

The Bottom Fisher

The Bottom Fisher is out there, right now, scouring the Web for deals. His desk is covered with every back-issue of every catalog from every mailing list in the country. An archaeologist would take a year to get to the bottom of all this crap. His in-box is full of emails from the Garagiste and Zachy's and Premier Cru, advising him of the latest offerings and the new items on sale. He is going to get the best price or die trying.

There are two kinds of Bottom Fishers: rich ones and Poor ones. Rich ones are better by far. The Rich Bottom Fisher is more interesting because he doesn't need to save any money. He's got plenty of that. What gets him off is stealing some wine for two-thirds of its market price. He has a list of everything he wants and the price he wants to pay, then he hunts it down with single-minded devotion like Elliot Ness.

He hangs around winebid.com and winecommune.com like a pedophile at a playground to see if he can sneak in bids with two minutes to go before the auction closes. He knows the guys at auction houses and picks up the lots that didn't sell for the reserve price—below the low estimate.

The Poor Bottom Fisher is someone to avoid with prejudice. He's got one hundred or one thousand bottles of wine, and none of them are any good. Instead of scouring the Internet (he's not going to pay for *shipping*), he spends his weekends scouring end-of-bin sales at liquor stores. He's always trying to introduce you to a fantastic six dollar bottle made from grape varietals you've never heard of—or from a country you didn't even know existed. "Really, I didn't think Petite Verdot would grow in Uzbeckistanislav."

The Perfectionist

There are only a few of these. It takes money, time, patience and money. (I mention money twice, because he'll need twice as much of that as he'll need of time and patience.) The Perfectionist is going to be constantly upgrading his cellar. He has no hesitation when it comes to "killing his children" (a chapter on this topic follows below) and trading wines that he's grown out of. One perfectionist is divesting himself of Pinots in favor of red Burgundies. He's already sold off his entire collection of Zinfandel and Merlot. The Chardonnays can't be far behind.

He is very thorough, with an accountant's sharp-pencil memory for figures. He knows where every bottle is. The Perfectionist is the one who sometimes points out typos in my inventory report. He is building something more than a wine collection; he is building a monument.

The Enthusiast

These guys are my favorites. They love it. They just love it. They love buying it and having it and talking about it and, most of all, sharing it with their friends. They love the friends they've made and continue to make through wine. They love the places they've gone because of it. My Enthusiast clients always have a lot of holes in the wall . . . and boxes on the floor.

The Enthusiast doesn't keep the receipts from the wine shop, but he does keep the special menus his wine group has enjoyed over the years. He loves seeing the wines in his collection mature and increase in value, and he mourns their eventual demise as if the bottles were old friends he hasn't seen enough of lately. Selling off wine, practical though it may be, is a difficult decision for this fellow. Getting the check is bittersweet, but then he buys some new things with the proceeds.

The Enthusiast takes his wine with him everywhere. He toasts any occasion, even the passing of a comrade-in-wine, with a great bottle because, "That's what it's there for."

The Fetishist

There's a store in LA called the Pleasure Chest that sells all kinds of vibrators and sex toys. I was there one night and saw something that looked like counterweights in a glass display case. Being a curious sort, I asked what they were used for. When the salesman explained their purpose, I said it sounded like that activity would be rather painful. He relocked the case and said: "Preference."

The Fetishist is the guy who, through a distinct palate or distinct financial conditions (either way), has established a preference for one or two things, to the exclusion of everything else. The rich Fetishist can afford to stay exclusively in older first growth Bordeaux and top white Burgundy wines. I have one client who has done exactly that, and not a single drop of wine from Italy, California or Australia sullies his racks. He just doesn't like any of it, because he feels it lacks history. While I was in his cellar I noticed one sad little bottle of red Burgundy sitting in a bin all by itself. When I pointed it out, he gave it to me—a 1989 Leroy Latricieres Chambertin with a price tag of around seven hundred dollars. Preference.

We have another friend who only drinks Burgundy, and even his fellow Burgundy-lovers question his single-minded devotion to the grape, asking, "Don't you get tired of it?" Honestly, it seems like if you ate lobster every night, you'd be begging for a hamburger. And so it goes.

The poor Fetishist is the one who can't afford to move up in class. He has an admirable collection of Zins and Syrahs, where the best values are to be had. The problem with the Poor Fetishist (again, the Rich one is better by far) is that he'll trot his fetish out wherever he goes. He brings a bottle of his best stuff to dinner, and it can be a bit embarrassing when the wine steward unscrews the cap. Do your own thing, man, let your freak flag fly, but do it behind closed doors. Get a room.

The Freak

Masters of Wine, known as MWs for short, are people who have studied and mastered a program as rigorous as any post-graduate doctorate—surgeons have it easier! There are only a few dozen MWs in the world. Set an unmarked glass of wine in front of a Master and he will place it on a certain bank of a certain river in a matter of moments. MWs are wine industry professionals whose breadth and depth of knowledge is astounding.

Then there are the other guys, the ones who do follow the Master's path without the benefit of compensation, and are essentially ranked amateurs. These Freaks are so wrapped up in their obsession; in the sports-analogy minutia of wine, the fluctuations in price of every wine on the market, knowing which wines are being released when, that you can't imagine they have time in their busy tasting schedule for other things—like a life. They seem to have already tasted everything and have an unshakeable opinion about all of it. Knowing a Freak is like having a source inside the locker room when you're trying to get a line on a game. They know all the little things, and never forget a detail, no matter how insignificant; they're dialed in. On the other hand, they can bore you to tears with weather reports from twenty years past and the nuances of malolactic fermentation. It can be like sitting with a boxing writer—you'd better really want to talk about the sweet science, or get another seat at the table.

The Banker

I have one client who demands his own category. He bought a bunch of wine with some other guys several years ago and they got some great things . . . in huge quantities. Twenty and Thirty cases *each* of Mouton and Margaux. They bought *en primeur*, paying around sixty dollars a bottle. Now it's twenty years later and these wines have appreciated six-fold. These few titles represent a quarter of his collection. I suggested that he should sell some off, but the

Banker explained to me that he deals in "relative values," and that these wines are now so valuable he can't afford to sell them. The way he figures it, the seller's commission would wipe out almost twenty percent of his ROI (return on investment), and he asked, "What am I going to get that's better for the price?"

"Diversity," I said.

The Banker is a guy who sees only dollar signs on wine labels. The wine is now so valuable that he can no longer enjoy it, won't open it and can't sell it. The only way he can get his full measure is to donate it to charity for the full current retail value, in exchange for a tax deduction.

I bring up the Banker because I believe that if you look at enough cellars, you can start to make certain assumptions about a person based on their wine collection. This guy's cellar had four thousand bottles valued at around a million dollars, but I didn't like it. I didn't like his approach to collecting, and I especially didn't like the way he was hoarding this stuff.

He also had what he called the "kids' cellar," a small area under the stairs, that we stocked with "everyday" wines—garden-variety stuff around twenty-five to thirty-five dollars per bottle. He was concerned that the wine we were allocating to the kids was too good. Talk about "relative value!"

6

Collecting

How Much Is Enough?

Thomas Jefferson once said, "Wine is a necessity." This is the same joker who came up with "all men are created equal," so you have to take everything he said or wrote with a grain of salt. Necessities are food, clothing and shelter. After those three come being in a band, writing a book, and wine. Wine is a necessity with a small *n*.

I went to a tasting of Penfolds Grange the other night. A reporter for the *Los Angeles Times* was covering the dinner and we started talking. I told her that you don't *need* wine. Nobody does. But it does add some light and flavor and spice and romance, and it introduces you to interesting people who share similar passions, and you *do* need those things in your life.

What's the perfect amount of wine? Part of the answer lies in your financial condition. Part lies in your ability to house it all properly. Part lies in your psychic make up. Taking these elements into account, you need as much wine as you can afford before it starts to ruin your life, your finances and your relationships. That is precisely how much you should buy.

In practical terms you need three hundred-and-sixty-five bottles a year—thirty cases. Multiply that by your life expectancy, and you've got the actual number of bottles you need. By that measure, I need 13,505 bottles (plus or minus) between now and when I go to the great wine cellar in the sky. You need more than you think. You need to have choices. Otherwise, the word *need* should never be part of the equation. It shouldn't even enter into the discussion. You need more than you can enjoy in your lifetime. A true collector is unhindered by logic.

My father turned seventy-five when the 2000 Bordeaux started rolling in. He bought twenty titles, maybe ten cases of wine that, according to almost everyone, would not be approachable for a dozen years or more. He'll be into his eighties, God willing, before he can open a single bottle, which makes it one of the most optimistic and ambitious acts in all of human history. He was not going to let something as insignificant as his impending dotage; actuarial tables predicting the approach of his ultimate demise, or the complete loss of his sense of taste deter him from his appointed rounds. I say: Bravo! Add to the equation the fact that he's already got over five thousand bottles, most of which are ready to drink. But my Dad could not stay away. That's what a collector *does*: He buys something he doesn't need, and may never live to enjoy, if only to keep his hand in the game.

I realize that my role as the organizer of other people's wine cellars makes me an enabler, a co-dependent of sorts. When I'm done putting things right, and after I've killed their children, they know two things: Exactly what they've got, and exactly how much room is left to fill. Paraphrasing the Beatles' *A Day in the Life*, "Now I know how many holes it takes to fill the Albert Hall because I had to count them all (I'd love to turn you on)."

How to Buy Wine

DO THE WORK: MAGAZINES

I have a client who is rapidly filling up his twenty-five hundred bottle cellar with great wines, mostly Bordeaux and Cabernets. He asked me how long it would take to learn all about wine. I told him that it's taken me forty-four years, and I'm just getting warm. Wine is like anything else that has history, nuance, and complexity: the more you know, the more you know how much you don't know.

You've got to do the work. It pays to read up on this stuff. Parker, the *Spectator*, Tanzer, *Decanter*, *Wine Enthusiast*, anything.

The cover of the current issue of *Wine Spectator* boasts "More Than 1,000 Wines Rated." The others are close. Reading them is a big help, as you can't possibly replicate the breadth of their findings. You'd have to give up your job in order to drink from morning 'til night.

Of course, you're now putting your own taste in the hands of a few experts. On the cover of every single issue of the *Wine Advocate*, Mr. Parker has a disclaimer that concludes: "However, there can never be any substitute for your own palate nor any better education than tasting the wine yourself."

It seems that there has been some "grade inflation" over the past few years, so that a score of 90 is the new 80. One client seems to think that a score in the high 80s is a solid "B," which means "very good" in school. Another client recently sold every bottle of wine that didn't rate 95 points from someone. Let me try to explain what they really mean by the 100-point scale.

100	Life altering, religious experience, chorus of angels singing
99	Mind boggling, rapturous, intense orgasm
98	Stupendous, brilliant, requires expletives
97	Awesome, stunning, tremendous
96	Fantastic, wonderful, eye-opening
95	Really, really great
94	Really great, delightful
93	Great, lovely, groovy
92	Very good, commendable, amusing
91	Good, pleasant, charming
90	On the cusp, feeling lucky to be here
89	The loneliest number in the game, near miss, no cigar
88	Better luck next time, out of the money
87	Drink up wine
86 & lower	Beer, please!

BOOKS

Have you ever read a book about wine? It's like reading about scuba diving. All that's missing is the part where you get wet and see the stuff for yourself. You may come away educated or entertained, but it hardly takes the place of being there and experiencing the thing first-hand. That said there are many wonderful books about wine written by people far more experienced in the field than I.

Unfortunately, I find that too many want to trace the origin of wine from ancient times to the current vintage, and offer tips on every damn thing under the sun, with quaint allegorical references to some experience the author had with . . . hey, wait a minute! I'm writing that book.

Most wine books are long on information and short on

entertainment. You want funny? Alexis Lichine ain't funny. Jay McInerney was funny before he started writing about wine, and Matt Kramer makes some funny analogies. Frank Prial in the *New York Times* can be funny, but Hugh Johnson ain't funny. Wine is serious business.

A list of my favorite wine books follows in the index.

CLASSES

Classes on wine are offered all over the country and many retailers organize tastings that are generally open to the public (you may have to call ahead to make a reservation) for around twenty to fifty dollars a person (sometimes more for better wines). Events such as these are worth attending because you really dissect each wine and learn the right terminology. Wine education classes are also offered at colleges and at the CIA (Culinary Institute) in Napa Valley and upstate New York.

If you ever get the chance to blend a wine, jump on it. Earlier this year I went up to Napa to make my own cuvee of Clark-Claudon Cabernet. The night before, I had dinner with some friends and told them how nervous I was—for all the time I spend with wine, I know nothing about blending it. It turns out that a few years ago ten of these friends had spent a day blending their own wines at Firestone Vineyards. Each guy made a case of his own secret formula. They said that the experience of blending had been illuminating and entertaining. The blending experiment culminated in one night when they got together over a steak dinner and tried all ten cuvees against one another in a tasting. They asked who else was going with my wife and I.

"Just us."

"Oh. How embarrassing," they said.

Where to Buy Wine

WINE STORES

Wine shops are interesting. The vagaries of state liquor laws mean that there are very few wine or liquor store chains and, as a result, wine shops have as much unique character as the stuff they sell. There are service-oriented shops with a fleet of trucks, and others that are self-serve grocery stores. Some are neighborhood joints with strong local clientele, while others are empty except for the UPS guy making his pick-up.

Wine shops are not like record stores: you can't walk in and expect to see the top one hundred on sale. Even the biggest shops carry only a fraction of the wines available. This can be a tremendous frustration to shoppers who have done their homework, made a list of the new wines they read about in the magazines, yet can't find any of them at the corner store. A client asked me what he should buy at a certain store, and all I could answer was "It depends on what they have to sell."

You've really got to get to know the people at the store. I spend a lot of time in wine shops, buying for clients or for myself. If you've got a good salesman who knows what you like and what your price point is, he'll get you in on the highly allocated new releases before they come in—and sell out.

DISTRIBUTION LISTS

I have a wine-loving friend who courts wine makers more ardently than he pursues women because he wants to get on the wine maker's distribution lists. He writes love letters and thank you notes to the wine makers. He reads wine magazines with a microscope to help fine-tune his plans for getting on the lists. There is a good reason for this single-mindedness, the hard-to-get California wines like Colgin and Turley and Kistler and Sine Qua Non are all sold exclusively (or nearly) through subscription lists. (These lists are an almost strictly American phenomenon.)

You should hear the cocks crowing about how they got to the top of the list, and the pathetic moans of those deemed unworthy. It's like getting a rejection letter from Harvard. Ann Colgin told me that she was offered a bribe of a new model Mercedes Benz for a spot on her list. (I don't know the end of the story, but she does drive a Mercedes.)

The yin and the yang of being on the list is that you have to order every year to stay on the list. The more you buy, the bigger your allotment, but then you're basically stuck with it in good years and bad. I have one client who's up to eight cases of Kistler Chardonnay. Now, Kistler Chardonnay is a very sought after wine, but purchasing it in that kind of quantity is a huge expense and requires practically a whole wing of the house to store it in. Still, I advised my client that it's better to take the eight cases and sell what you don't need to friends than to lose your spot on the list.

The other thing to watch out for is that you have to earn the good stuff. Turley makes about a dozen different single-vineyard Zinfandels and Petite Syrahs. The most sought-after are Hayne, Moore and Aida, but you're likely to have to take a case of their somewhat lesser wines to merit a single bottle of any of these.

Finally, some people get on the mailing list of one producer and are practically overrun with one wine, to the exclusion of almost everything else. One client had every title from Behrens & Hitchcock (and they make a lot of single vintages), which isn't bad, but there's more to life—unfortunately, there's no more room in his cellar.

AUCTIONS

Wine shops charge a premium for older offerings, so if you're going to buy older vintages, your best bet is the auction game. Live auctions are exhilarating and stressful; I often bid on wines for more than one client, sometimes wielding two paddles. I may go into the auction with some kind of bidding strategy, but it's tough to stick to those parameters once the game gets under way. The stress of an important auction can get so overwhelming that I almost prefer to send in absentee bids and find out how I did the next day—like casting a vote in an election, or buying a lottery ticket.

Auction buyers need three things: dedication, discipline and decisiveness. Dedication because these catalogs can be the size of a small-town phone book and take time to read through. The recent Zachys catalog weighed in at 245 pages, with nearly 2000 lots to consider. You must be prepared for the show before the action starts; Discipline because it's easy to get caught up in the drama of the action in the room. A paddle is a dangerous weapon in the wrong hands; and Decisiveness because you've got to establish a game plan and a budget—either for each lot or a grand total you want to spend—and stick with it.

You've got to pay to play, my friends. Christie's, Zachy's, Sotheby's, et. al charge hefty subscription fees for their auction catalogs, most of which are not available online. And keep in mind that the friendly-looking estimates quoted in the catalog don't take into account the buyer's premium (usually 15 to 20 percent) mandatory insurance (1 percent), storage fees, tax or delivery.

One further caveat: It pays to investigate the provenance of the wine. The catalogs typically say that the wine is being offered from "the estate of a gentleman" or "has been stored under optimal conditions since release." The more they go on about the cellar conditions the better, but it is still no guarantee that the wines were adequately cellared. To be fair, you don't know how a store is keeping their wine either, but you can build a relationship with your local dealer who will then be more likely to take something back to keep your business. You do have the opportunity to inspect (and even reject) wine bought at auction before taking possession of it, and I recommend that you do.

ONLINE

With the advent of the Internet the amount of wine information available to the average person has exploded, and as a result there has never a better time to be a wine buyer than right now. The Internet has transformed the once provincial nature of wine retailing; there's nothing you can't find with a couple of clicks.

You will never be lonely once you register for some of these sites. I get about a dozen emails every day from the likes of Sokolin, Premier Cru, Garagiste, *TheWineBroker.com*, Zachy's and others. These guys are the Will Rogers of wine; they never met a bottle of wine they didn't like. They somehow manage to say something good about every bottle of fermented grape juice that comes across the transom, but if you take the time actually read their spam, you'll be ahead of the crowd on the best deals.

A word of advice: Do not tarry. A lot of these offerings are priced to move and a delay of a few hours can be enough time for the wine to sell out. You never want to hear, "I'm sorry."

How Not to Buy Wine: Clubs & Grocery Stores

The only time I ever look at the wine selections in a grocery store is when I need something to stash in the cooking-wine section of my cellar. There are exceptions to this rule, of course, but I believe if you can buy a bottle of wine along with a carton of eggs, that bottle probably does not belong in the company of serious wine except as an ingredient in the Coq au Vin. I like to check them out just to make sure they never make an appearance in one of my cellars.

The other place not to buy wine from is a wine club. I got a mailer the other day from an outfit that came on to me like a cheap hooker. It seems I was *pre-approved as a charter member! No minimum purchase required!* (I'm sure if Groucho Marx were alive, he wouldn't want to be pre-approved as a member either.) A *Free!* welcome gift was waiting for me. Crap. The wine club promised rare gems "that we simply can't make available to all members." Crap. You get more free crap if you help them recruit more clients into their Ponzi scheme.

A recent Wall Street Journal story said that a lot of the "rare gems" they promise are actually re-packaged surplus wine they try to fob off as a "private label." And, to make matters worse, you're not necessarily getting a better price on this crap than you would at the store.

Not all wine clubs are bad news. I started my own wine club, called Liquid Assets, with five other guys. Each of us invested three thousand dollars. I buy the wine and keep track of the accounting, which I post online. We set the average bottle price at fifty dollars although the actual price for the first go-round was closer to forty-five dollars, with no specific guidelines as to what I should buy. Our first "shareholder's meeting" was held at AOC, a hot new wine bar in L.A. that serves up small portions and offers one hundred wines by the glass (none of which we tried that night). Each couple got one plate to split, paired with a different wine with each of the seven courses, working our way up the flavor scale with each course. At the end of the night, I gave everyone two mixed cases of wine, including everything we'd had that evening. I try to make sure that everything is approachable by the time I mete it out.

Much as I dislike the garden-variety wine club, this one works because I'm watching the market for sales, and I have access to a lot of information. I do the work and everybody benefits. We seldom overpay. Indeed, we saw a 38 percent price increase over a one-year period, and all the shareholders came back for a second year. I only buy wines that I would drink, and I like to think that I set the bar pretty high. While it's possible that someone might not like any one of the wines, I work hard to make sure that everything on the list is an outstanding representation of the varietal. A wine club such as this is a great opportunity to try wines outside of your "comfort zone;" for instance most of the group was surprised to find how much they liked the Spanish wines.

7

What to Buy: The Balanced Collection

The best collections have balance, and every collector strikes his own balance that reflects his personality and taste. Every collection is as unique as a snowflake. One of the best parts of my job is the sense of discovery I feel unfolding the distinct character of each cellar.

While writing this chapter, struggling with the impossibility of advising some stranger on the composition of their *Best Cellar*, I went to a wine tasting dinner with a big television executive who knew nothing about wine. The host poured great stuff, and the TV Exec turned to me and asked: "How much for a wine cellar?" I didn't hesitate to say that a one thousand bottle cellar would put him "in the game," and the total cost, including the design, construction and the wine would come to one hundred and fifty thousand dollars. I was guessing. I guessed right. The cellar is now under construction, and we're going shopping.

The next several pages detail what I think would make for the *Best Cellar*. I doubt that any individual collector would agree that this is the perfect snowflake for them, but it reflects a cross-section of wines, and allows for both breadth and depth. Every collector has to follow his own star. I applaud my client who was blown away by some Rhone wines at a friend's barbeque and sold all his Bordeaux and Cabs the next day. Just up and swapped them for Pinots and Rhones. Bravo! He did the right thing for himself and his changing tastes.

The top ten wines listed in each category are perennially the most collectible and most sought after wines, and often the most rare and expensive. I don't claim that these are the best, just the ones I see most often in the best cellars.

France

BORDEAUX

The *Best Cellars* are almost always rich in Bordeaux; they are among the greatest names in wine, and a case study in why cellaring wines is worthwhile. A quick look at Parker's assessment of the great 2000 Bordeaux vintage suggests that, for the most part, they will not be ready to be enjoyed fully for at least seven years. Some will not achieve maturity for a decade or more. As good as the 2000s look on paper, the 1990s are much more pleasurable to drink now.

Forget most white wines from Bordeaux. The Haut Brion Blanc

and Laville Haut Brion have a following, but the majority of Bordeaux wine makers haven't really invested themselves in making a world-class white wine, so why should you invest in it?

The Top Ten Collectible Bordeaux are:

1. Petrus
2. Latour
3. Lafite-Rothschild
4. Lafleur
5. Haut Brion
6. Margaux
7. Cheval Blanc
8. Le Pin
9. Mouton-Rothschild
10. Leoville Las Cases

BURGUNDY

I have a client with a substantial Bordeaux collection of good-vintage first-growths and Pomerols worth about one hundred and fifty thousand dollars. Recently he advised me that he wants to get into Burgundy, and could I help him. I wrote him back, saying that his request was like asking for a couple of good Classical CD recommendations, or, could I tell him about baseball? Where do you even begin? Beyond that, even though I know what this guy pays for Bordeaux (his average bottle price is valued at over one hundred and fifty dollars), I warned him to expect sticker-shock if he got into high end Burgundies. I told him to start with some DRC, some Jayers and Leroys, and see if he's still hungry for more after he gets the bill. You'd better really love this stuff because it's a slippery slope once you get started.

The Top Eleven Collectible Burgundies producers are:

1. DRC: Domaine Romanee-Conti (In order of importance: Romanee-Conti, La Tache, Richebourg, Grands Echezeaux, Echezeaux, Romanee-St. Vivant)
2. Domaine Leroy (Clos de Vougeot, Clos de la Roche, Latricieres Chambertin, Richebourg, Romanee-St. Vivant, Nuits St. Georges Aux Boudots)
3. Henri Jayer (especially the Vosne Romanee Cros Parantoux and Echezeaux)
4. Comte Georges de Vogue (Musigny Vieilles Vignes and Bonnes Mares)
5. Anne Gros Richebourg (There are several Gros family members all making good wine)
6. Claude Dugat (Charmes / Griotte / Gevrey-Chambertin)
7. Camille Giroud
8. Hubert Lignier (Clos de la Roche)
9. Joseph Roty (Charmes-Chambertin)
10. Bouchard Pere et Fils (La Romanee)
11. Dujac (Clos de la Roche)

RHONE

At a recent dinner party I attended one of the guests wanted to impress his boss with a bottle of wine. He brought a bottle of Guigal Cote-Rotie, La Mouline 1999. An objective observer (that would be me), said, "Winner! Turkey dinner!"

The boss, somewhat harder to impress, admitted, "It's not chopped liver."

Rhone wines are undergoing a remarkable renaissance, and many educated collectors count these as their favorites.

The Top Twelve Collectible Rhone wines are:

1. Guigal Cote-Rotie La Turque
2. Guigal Cote-Rotie La Landonne

3. Guigal Cote-Rotie La Mouline
4. Beaucastel Chateauneuf-du-Pape Hommage a Jacques Perrin
5. Jaboulet Hermitage La Chapelle
6. Domaine de la Mordoree Chateauneuf-du-Pape Cuvee la Reine des Bois
7. Chateau Rayas Reserve
8. Chave Hermitage
9. Chapoutier Ermitage Le Pavillon
10. Chapoutier Ermitage L'Ermite
11. Les Cailloux Cuvee Centenaire
12. Pegau Chateauneuf-du-Pape Cuvee da Capo

Italy

Despite what many new collectors think, Brunello di Montalcino did not invent Italian wine in 1997. This perception began after the *Wine Spectator* put the 1997 vintage on its cover and gave every Brunello wine a score in the mid-nineties. Most of them cost in the very reasonable thirty to sixty dollar range, so people went absolutely ape. I don't want to crash the party, but a lot of this was really just hype. A friend heard a very perceptive comment at a tasting of 1990 Brunellos (Brunelli?), when one of the guests admitted, "I think we're trying too hard to love these wines." Don't get me wrong, they're pretty good, but in Italy they don't even medal. Twenty-five years ago there was only one producer making these wines (Biondi Santi).

The real collectors go after Barolo, Barbaresco (the King and Queen, respectively), and the so-called Super-Tuscans (almost anything ending in "aia" is good: Ornellaia, Solaia, Sassicaia), all of which are both more substantial, and substantially more expensive.

White wines from Italy are good for drinking but not for cellaring. My wife calls Pinot Grigio "colored water." They're fun and light and perfect for a hot summer day, but they're not built to last much longer than the trip from the store to your house. I have several clients with one thousand or more bottles of Italian wine, and not a drop of it is white. If you like the stuff, buy it a case at a time and keep it near the front door of the cellar because it isn't going to be staying there long.

BAROLO

The Top Ten Collectible Barolos are:

1. Gaja Sperss
2. Aldo Conterno Granbussia (only produced in great vintages).
3. Giacomo Conterno Monfortino Riserva
4. Voerzio La Morra
5. Ceretto Bricco Rocche
6. Clerico Ciabot Mentin Ginestra
7. Aldo Conterno Riserva
8. Bruno Giacosa Le Rocche
9. Pio Cesare Ornato
10. Paolo Scavino Bric del Fiasc

BARBARESCO

The Top Five Collectible Barbarescos are:

1. Gaja Sori San Lorenzo
2. Gaja Sori Tilden
3. Aldo Conterno Riserva
4. Bruno Giacosa Sori Tildin
5. Bruno Giacosa Asili

SUPER TUSCANS

The Top Ten Collectible Super Tuscans:

1. Sassicaia
2. Masseto
3. Ornellaia
4. Solaia
5. Tignanello
6. Solengo Argiano
7. Castello dei Rampolla Sammarco
8. Flaccianello Fontodi
9. Ceparello Isole e Olena
10. Montevertine Le Pergole Torte or Il Soldaccio

BRUNELLO DI MONTALCINO

The Top Ten Collectible Brunello di Montalcino:

1. Altesino Montosoli
2. Ciacci Piccolomini
3. Pian delle Vigne (Antinori)
4. CastelGiacondo (Frescobaldi)
5. Casanova di Neri
6. Caparzo La Casa
7. Soldera Case Basse or Intistieti
8. Biondi Santi (The Originator)
9. Poggio Antico
10. Lisini

OTHER

The Top Ten Collectible "Other" Italian wines:

1. Gaja Costa Russi
2. Tua Rita Reddigaffi
3. Dal Forno Romano Amarone TB
4. Allegrini Amarone

5. Gaja Darmaji Cabernet Sauvignon
6. Braida Ai Suma Barbera d'Asti
7. Fattoria di Felsina Berardegna Chianti Classico
8. Masi Amarone
9. Voerzio Barbera d'Alba Riserva
10. Quintarelli Giuseppe Reciotto

California

CABERNET SAUVIGNON & CABERNET BLENDS

The wines that put Napa Valley on the map are still the gold standard, but are now among the worst values in the market. The market has gone crazy on high-end cult Cabs, and the Two-Buck Chucks* are capturing the bottom end, leaving the middle wide open. The lack of good-to-great Cabs under sixty dollars has made other varietals more attractive to the average consumer. Nevertheless, these are the undisputed Kings of California wine, and an integral part of *The Best Cellar*.

The Top Ten Collectible Cabernet Sauvignons and Cabernet Blends (and the twenty runners-up) are:

1. Screaming Eagle (although there is not a living soul who thinks it's worth the price)
2. Harlan Estate
3. Colgin (Herb Lamb Vineyard, Tychson Hill Vineyard, Cariad)
4. Araujo Eisele Vineyard

....

* *"Two Buck Chuck" is the nickname for Charles Shaw wines that sell for $1.99 at Trader Joe's markets in California. They are wildly popular, and "Two Buck Chuck" has become a catch-all phrase for very inexpensive wines.*

5. Joseph Phelps Insignia
6. Chateau Montelena Estate
7. Caymus Special Selection
8. Shafer Hillside Reserve
9. Dominus Estate
10. Dunn Howell Mountain (the bloom is, sadly, off the rose)
11. Pride Mountain Reserve
12. Heitz Martha's Vineyard (It ain't what it used to be)
13. Clark-Claudon
14. Opus One
15. Peter Michael Les Pavots
16. Pahlmeyer
17. Ridge Monte Bello
18. Beringer Private Reserve
19. B.V. Private Reserve
20. Robert Mondavi Reserve
21. Chateau St. Jean Cinq Cepages
22. Diamond Creek (Gravelly Meadow, Red Rock Terrace, Volcanic Hill)
23. Behrens & Hitchcock
24. Abreu
25. Flora Springs (Rutherford Hillside Reserve & Triology)
26. Silver Oak (in order: Napa Valley and Alexander Valley)
27. Lewis Cellars (Cuvee L and Reserve)
28. Leonetti Cellars Reserve
29. Lokoya (Diamond Mountain, Mt. Veeder and Howell Mountain)
30. Philip Togni

MERLOT

While I was writing this book, the *Wine Spectator* selected the Paloma Merlot 2000 as their Wine of the Year. Much as I want *The Best Cellar* to be favorably reviewed in that estimable journal, I feel it's my responsibility to point out the distinct possibility that they have all lost their minds over there.

I had dinner with Christian Moieux of Dominus recently. His family also owns a little property in Bordeaux called Chateau Petrus, which makes what is almost universally acknowledged to be the greatest merlot-based wine in the world. He told me that he's tearing out all the merlot vines in Napa Valley because he doesn't believe it's possible to grow "great" merlot there. He ought to know.

The notion of a "great California Merlot" is an oxymoron.

I think people just like saying the word *Merlot*. It sounds nice. It sounds exotic. "I'll have a glass of Merlot, please."

My friend Kimberly Jones has a way of anthropomorphizing her description of wines. She once said a Cabernet was like the "silk buttons on a satin dress." Another, older Bordeaux evoked memories of waking up to find a guy making pancakes on a rainy morning. I never know what the hell she's talking about, but I got the feeling she was not partial to Merlot when she said that drinking them is "like licking a scab." I could be wrong.

Players look down their noses at Merlot. It is not a wine that merits serious cellaring. Hackers have them in quantity, but mostly I think they're bar wines. There are truly great Merlots, but they're made in other countries. Petrus, Le Pin, Lafleur, are all merlot-based wines from Pomerol in Bordeaux. These are insanely expensive wines. (A sommelier told me about a customer who came into his restaurant and ordered a Bordeaux wine, but insisted that they did not want a Cabernet or a Merlot. The Bordeaux they ordered was made almost exclusively from those two grapes, as are most Bordeaux. Troglodytes.) Italy makes a handful of collectible Merlots, including Masseto, Castello di Ama, and Fallesco Montiano.

It seems that making a really good, balanced Merlot is harder than hitting a knuckle ball. The grape is used for blending in so many wines, but as the major ingredient, it generally doesn't seem to work. It's like hiring a character actor to star in your summer blockbuster. It's all out of place in such a big role. Imagine if Eli Wallach had Clint Eastwood's roles. You need guys like Eli to fill out your cast, but maybe Clint would be better in the lead, after all. That said, these are the best of the bunch.

The Top Ten Collectible Merlots are:

1. Pahlmeyer
2. Pride Mountain
3. Beringer Bancroft Ranch
4. Duckhorn (resting on their laurels after establishing the benchmark in the 90s)
5. Lewis Reserve
6. Paloma
7. Leonetti Cellars
8. Robert Sinskey Reserve
9. Newton Unfiltered
10. Behrens & Hitchcock Reserve

PINOT NOIR

Some think American Pinot is the poor man's poor substitute for Burgundy. My father, who is a just and fair person, says, "Why would I drink Pinot Noir?" This was proven to me at a Burgundy tasting recently held at Spago. Only wines from the good years: '90, '93 and '96, were represented. However, one participant whose collection is concentrated in California wine brought a bottle of the Kistler Cuvee Elizabeth, their Big Kahuna. Parker gave it 98 points. It sells for three hundred dollars a bottle. The sommelier slipped it into the third flight and announced that there was a spy in our midst. Of course, the color of the Pinot gave it away from ten paces, and I didn't wait until the glasses got to the table before I called out the imposter. The others disdainfully nosed it out and quickly and harshly dismissed it. I'm pretty sure that this wine would be very good on its own, and might even shine among other Pinots, but in the company of Chambertins and Vosne-Romanees it paled by comparison. During the onslaught the hapless Pinot bearer, who is both a friend and a client, leaned over to me and whispered, "Dump the Pinots."

Yet perhaps the comparison is unfair, after all people go nuts for the American Pinots. I think the quality of Pinot, especially those produced in Santa Barbara County and in Oregon, has improved enormously in the past few years, and a genuine "New World" style has emerged.

The Top Ten Collectible Pinot Noirs are:

1. Marcassin
2. Williams Selyem
3. Kistler
4. Sine Qua Non
5. Rochioli
6. Domaine Drouhin
7. Brewer-Clifton
8. Au Bon Climat
9. Martinelli
10. Bonaccorsi (Sadly, these have become more collectible in the wake of Michael Bonaccorsi's untimely death)

SYRAH

I'm going to go out on a limb here, but not too far: the most exciting wines being produced on three continents right now are Syrah-based wines, also called Rhone blends. The *Wine Spectator* did an entire issue on the subject. Production is way up. Winemakers are pulling out their Merlot vines (Hallelujah!) and replacing them with Syrah. The best values in the wine world today are in Rhone and Australian Syrahs, and Syrahs are where the action is among California wines. They're big, sweaty, spicy meatballs.

The Top Ten Collectible Syrahs (in the U.S.) are:

1. Sine Qua Non (the name changes every year, most recently Midnight Oil)
2. Araujo
3. Alban
4. Pax (several single vineyards, all instant sell-outs)
5. Colgin (this is a prediction; their first release is due out soon)
6. Kongsgaard
7. Lewis Cellars
8. Qupe
9. Ojai (Roll Ranch, Stolpman Vineyard, Bien Nacido Vineyard)
10. Dehlinger

ZINFANDEL

I have one client whose entire collection is from California. He has two sad little bottles of Bordeaux that a well-meaning business associate gave him, but otherwise his collection is all from just up the coast. He's into it. He's really, really into it. He wants to talk about it all the time. He wants to get together and open a bottle tonight. I love guys like him because they want to learn and drink and share.

This guy is doing all right. He's not super-rich, like some of my clients. He doesn't live behind gates. He got into wine a little while ago, befriended a guy at the local wine shop and started putting together a collection based on getting the most bang-for-the-buck. Among American wines, the best deals are in varietals. The top Cabernets and Cab Blends are getting out of sight of the average consumer, but you can get a bunch of Zins and Syrahs for under fifty dollars. These are some of the most exciting, vibrant, hedonistic, slutty wines available. Parker says: "Zinfandel remains popular because it is distinctively California, and can be immensely satisfying. But it is never a 'great' wine." The greatest:

The Top Ten Collectible Zinfandels are:

1. Turley Hayne Vineyard
2. Turley Moore Earthquake Vineyard
3. Martinelli Jackass Vineyard
4. Turley (pick one)
5. Ridge*
6. Seghesio
7. Rosenblum*
8. Rabbit Ridge*
9. Ravenswood*
10. Rochioli*

Australia

The most fun place to shop. These wines tend to be so big, concentrated, dense and alcoholic that I drink them more by themselves as a cocktail than with food except with a big hunk of steak or something spicy.

Most Australian wines are not built to last. Penfolds Grange and Henschke Hill of Grace are obvious exceptions, and there are others that merit extended cellaring, but most will be at their best within five years of the vintage. There has been a lot of talk lately about some very highly rated Australian wines and their aging potential. Christian Navarro, the "Sommelier to the Stars" at Wally's wine

....

* *In his book Bacchus and Me, Jay McInerney says that any Zin starting with the letter "R" is probably good.*

shop in LA, suggests that a lot of people who spent a lot of money on these wines are going to be sadly disappointed in a few years when they find that a lot of the fun went out of them. Place your bets.

The Top Eleven Collectible Australian Wines are:

1. Penfolds Grange
2. Henschke Hill of Grace
3. Three Rivers Dry Grown Shiraz
4. Torbreck Run Rig
5. Greenock Creek Roenfeldt Road (Cabernet and Shiraz)
6. Noon (Eclipse, Reserve Cabernet and Reserve Shiraz)
7. Clarendon Hills Astralis
8. Kay Brothers Block 6
9. Fox Creek Reserve
10. Marquis Philips "Integrity"
11. D'Arenberg Wines

Spain

Spanish wines have been overlooked for years, but this is finally changing. Riojas, Ribera del Dueros and Toros are coming into their own on the world stage. From a collector's standpoint, there is Vega Sicilia Unico, and then there is everything else. It is made only in great years, released a decade or more after the vintage, and has no peer.

The more adjectives you have describing Spanish wine the better. Gran Riserva Espciale is better than Gran Riserva, which, in turn, is better than a Riserva—all of which designates how long the wine was aged in both oak and the bottle before release.

The Top Ten Collectible Spanish Wines are:

1. Vega Sicilia Unico
2. Pingus
3. Castillo y Gay
4. Numanthia Torremanthia
5. Torre Muga
6. Cune Rioja Reserva
7. Pesquera Gran Riserva Especiale
8. L'Ermita Priorat
9. Muga Prado Enea Rioja Gran Reserva
10. Rioja Alta Viña Arana

White Wines

Here's a good rule: No more than five to ten percent of your collection should be white wines. That percentage should come down as your collection grows. Most whites don't age well beyond five years (some Rieslings, Rhones and white Burgundy wines stand out as exceptions), so you don't want to get too heavily committed to wines that almost demand to be opened tomorrow, or the next day.

My wife doesn't like Chardonnay. She is, unwittingly perhaps, at the forefront of a Chardonnay-bashing movement. She doesn't like the sharp oakiness or the buttery flavors. When I met her, she drank Pinot Grigio, which was one of those good news/bad news scenarios. The good news was that most Pinot Grigio costs around ten dollars a bottle. (The most famous one, Santa Margherita, is the single most popular imported wine in America, and goes for about twice that, but is not noticeably better—a triumph of marketing.) The bad news was that if we continued to have a relationship, I was going to be seen in the company of Pinot Grigio entirely too often. Not that there's anything wrong with it on a hot summer day, ideally on the Amalfi coast, but I wouldn't want my daughter to date one, if you know what I mean.

It has been a great adventure trying to find viable alternatives. White Burgundy is an obvious choice, because even though most are made of Chardonnay grapes and aged in oak, they have a completely different flavor, body and greater complexity than most American models. When a California Chardonnay is praised, it is almost always with the modifier "Burgundian." The problem with White Burgundy wines is the price tag. You can noodle around Chablis and Meursault on a budget, but anything that ends in the word "Montrachet" is likely to be *tres chere*.

The Top Eleven Collectible White Burgundies are:

1. DRC Montrachet
2. Lafon Montrachet
3. Coche Dury Corton-Charlemagne
4. Sauzet Montrachet
5. Louis Latour Montrachet
6. Jadot Montrachet
7. Joseph Drouhin Montrachet Marquis de Laguiche
8. Colin-Deleger Montrachet
9. Henri Boillot Montrachet
10. Bouchard Pere et Fils Le Montrachet
11. Ramonet Montrachet

The Top Ten Collectible Chardonnays:

1. Marcassin
2. Aubert (Ritchie and Quarry Vineyards)
3. Peter Michael (all of them, but especially Belle Cote)
4. Pahlmeyer
5. Kistler (several single vineyards—all good)
6. Kongsgaard
7. Patz & Hall Alder Springs

8. Shafer (Red Shoulder Ranch)
9. Leeuwin Estate Art Series (Australia)
10. Stony Hill (subscription only)

The Top Eight Sauvignon Blancs—with the caveat that Sauvignon Blancs are not truly "collectible," and should be bought season to season. These are the ones I see most often in the *Best Cellars*:

1. Peter Michael L'Apres Midi
2. Araujo
3. Mayacamas
4. Crocker & Starr
5. Cloudy Bay (New Zealand)
6. Duckhorn
7. Spottswoode
8. Groth

The Top Five Collectible Austrian White Wine Producers are*:

1. Franz Hirtzberger Riesling Singerriedel
2. FX Pichler Gruner Veltliner "M"
3. Prager Riesling Klaus
4. Knoll Gruner Veltliner Loibner Vinotekfullung
5. Nagl

Other White Wines:

1. Sine Qua Non (they change the name every year, most recently Albino, Whisperin' E, and Sublime Isolation)
2. Ott Rose
3. Tavel Rose
4. Araujo Viognier

....

*Each producer has a line of several Gruner Veltliners and Rieslings. Only the most highly collectible is listed.

Champagne*

Champagne is the most affordable luxury in the world. A G-4 is twenty-five million dollars. A serious car is six figures. A bottle of Cristal is about a $125. The Queen of England doesn't drink better champagne than I do. Relatively, the best champagne in the world is a bargain.

I am always disappointed to see a well-stocked cellar with no champagne. When I get done with my inventory, I put together some statistical charts and graphs to show the client exactly what he's got and quite often the missing link is Champagne. Don't these people plan to celebrate anything soon? Are they going to thrill to the sound of a cork popping from a bottle of sparkling cider?

Rule number one of wine collecting: The most important bottle in any collection is the bottle of champagne you keep in the refrigerator, because you never know when you're going to want to celebrate something.

Showy champagnes are expensive, which is why rap stars like them, and there's no questioning the quality of the top names. There are plenty of great champagnes for forty to sixty dollars, every bit as good, but not likely to earn you props with your posse of homeboyz unless they know what they're doing.

The Top Ten Collectible Big Bucks Champagnes are:

1. Krug Clos du Mesnil
2. Dom Perignon (Moet et Chandon)
3. Cristal (Louis Roederer)
4. Taittinger Comte de Champagne Rose
5. Veuve Clicquot La Grande Dame

....

  * *California champagne is not champagne. It is sparkling wine or, in a pathetic display of Franco-envy, Methode Champenoise. Some of it is more than passable, but you won't impress anyone with the label.*

6. Salon Le Mesnil
7. Krug Vintage
8. Bollinger RD
9. Gosset Grand Millesime
10. Laurent-Perrier Grand Siecle

Dessert Wines

A few months ago my wife and I threw a dinner party and had every guest bring a bottle of wine. We were having a lot of fun until one of the couples got into a big argument about whether the husband should go get another bottle from the car to have with dessert. The bottle was a 1939 Coutet dessert wine from Barsac. It had belonged to his late father, and was being saved for a toast at his youngest daughter's wedding. The husband reasoned that his daughter might not get married for another twenty-five years and that he might not live long enough to enjoy it. The men adjourned to the kitchen to open it—very, very carefully. The color of the wine had turned a rich caramel brown over sixty-five years. We poured a little bit into a glass to see if it was still any good and passed the glass around. I looked into the faces of the others as smiles lit up their faces, tears welled up in their eyes, laughter and shrieks of joy filled the air. It was mind-boggling. The finish went on so long that I got goose bumps. Meanwhile, the women were in the other room, talking about how insensitive the men were to drink up their ten-year-old daughter's wedding wine.

What is better than dessert wine? Nothing! Skip dessert. Drink dessert. Dessert wines should be one of the smallest, but not the least important section of your collection, making up three to eight percent of the total bottles.

SAUTERNES

Sauternes, especially Chateau d'Yquem, are probably the gold standard; as Laurel Margerum of the Wine Cask in Santa Barbara said, "Yquem is so indescribably delicious that it must be made from a fruit that doesn't exist." Young Sauternes can be great, but if you are one of the few lucky ones who can save them for a long, long time, an old Sauternes is one of the greatest things in the world.

The Top Ten Collectible Sauternes are:

1. Yquem
2. Rieussec
3. Guiraud
4. Climens
5. Nairac
6. Lafaurie-Peyraguey
7. Suduiraut
8. Raymond Lafon
9. Doisy Daene "L'Extravagant"
10. La Tour Blanche

PORT

You don't need a lot of port. You can't drink a lot of port. Port is a wine that fairly demands an occasion and enough people to appreciate it. In his book *Bacchus and Me,* Jay McInerney says, "It's never a good idea to pour a third glass of port, no matter how good the plan seems at the time. And even a second glass should not be undertaken lightly by those who hope to get lucky, or to drive home."

The problem with port, for a lot of people, is that it should be twenty-five years old before you open it. I disagree. I stopped by Wally's, the venerable wine shop in Westwood, one Saturday when they were having a ten-dollar tasting of ports, including the Taylor Fladgate 2000, one of the top-rated wines from a top-rated vintage.

It was fantastic, complex, overwhelming, and completely enjoyable. Not as refined as the '77, but I don't think most people turn to Port for its subtlety. You want to get your ass kicked. You've already had a bunch of wine by the time you get to the port and your taste buds are screaming for something to wash down the Stilton, or the cigar—or at least put up a fair fight.

One good thing about vintage Port is that it's an easy area to master. There are only a handful of top producers, and they only put out wine in years that merit a vintage bottling, almost all of which are worthwhile as collectibles.

The Top Ten Collectible Ports are:
1. Taylor Fladgate
2. Graham's
3. Warre's
4. Dow's
5. Fonseca
6. Quinta do Noval (especially the Nacionale)
7. Croft
8. Quinta do Vesuvio
9. Sandeman
10. Niepoort

The top recent vintages are: '63, '70, '77, '94, '97 and '00.

One note—I see vintage Port on the by-the-glass menu quite often, which means that it may have been open for several days. Even though it's been fortified, vintage port doesn't keep better than other wine once it's been uncorked. It will oxidize and get a little prune-y on the nose and lose its brilliance after a day or two. Better to ask when the bottle was opened and be thought a wine snob than not to ask and be a fool. (Tawny Port keeps forever. It was made in a way that further oxidation won't adversely affect it.)

OTHERS

There are lots of other really fantastic dessert wines, many of them German Trockenbeerenausleses, with names even more improbable to pronounce and spell.

The Top Ten Collectible non-Sauternes Dessert Wines are:

1. Kracher Numbers 1-12
2. J.J. Prum
3. Sine Qua Non "Mr. K" series (made in association with Alois Kracher)
4. Inniskillin Ice Wine. "Ice Wine" is translated from the German "Eiswein." Those Canadians are sooo clever.
5. Dolce (produced by Nickel & Nickel)
6. Avignonesi Vin Santo
7. Felluga Picolit
8. Tirecul La Gradiere Monbazillac Cuvee Madame
9. Zind Humbrecht Tokay Pinot Gris Clos Windsbuhl
10. Selbach Oster Riesling Eiswine Bernkasteler Badstube

When Should I Drink It?

Ninety-five percent of wine is consumed within three hours of leaving the store. These are called "drink-up" wines. You've no doubt heard that beautiful women get "better with age, like a fine wine," but you've probably never hear about the toothless old hags who aged like cheap wines. The truth of it is that most wines aren't very good and they're not built to last. Those aren't the wines we're dealing with here.

I have a client who is afraid of his wine. He's afraid that it will be either too early or too late to open the bottle and, either way, he will have missed the perfect moment. He's absolutely right.

Deciding when to open a bottle is something like deciding when to pull the starting pitcher from a baseball game. Pull him too soon and you may never find out what else he's got to give—an opportunity lost. Wait too long and the game may be over—the writing was on the wall. If the Red Sox had pulled Pedro Martinez when I said they should, they would have been dancing in the streets of Kenmore Square one year earlier and the manager would still have his job, but that's beside the point. That's the thing about wine: you don't know except by tasting, reading and *kibitzing*. It doesn't come with an expiration date on the back label. I've heard someone say that collecting old Burgundies is like owning a vintage Jaguar. It might just break down on the side of the road one day. You pays your money and you takes your chances.

On the other hand, there's my mother-in-law, Mimi. She had some romantic encounter at Chateau Lynch Bages one time, and it remains her favorite wine. She has a case of the '98, an indifferent vintage at best, but she trots it out like some great trophy. It's 2005 and the official betting line on this wine is that it won't achieve its indifferent status for another three years. Until then, it's horrible. I had lunch with Jean-Michel Cozes, the owner of Lynch Bages not long ago. I told Mimi that Monsieur Cozes said, "Quel horreur!" and stated absolutely that she must not open another bottle of this vintage until 2007. I'm pleased to announce that my intervention has thus pre-empted another unfortunate international incident between the Americans and the French. (I asked Monsieur Cozes which was his favorite vintage of Lynch Bages. He said, "The one I have to sell!")

That's why the pop of a cork is one of the most enduring and endearing sounds in the human experience. There's a mystery being unraveled inside. (There's a reason they don't write songs about vodka, you know.) That sound is the genie coming out of the bottle. The most common advice I give clients is to drink from back to front. Start getting into all those older wines, because if you don't, you'll miss them when they're gone. And that, my friends, would be a tragedy.

I offer the following caveat to my clients along with their Carte du Vin, the scores and suggested *Hold 'Til* and *Drink By* dates: The guidelines Parker and the *Spectator* offer are pretty good, but you may prefer your wine either younger or more mature. Listen to your palate. I don't know how, based on a barrel sample of a coltish Cabernets being tasted side-by-side with forty others in one seating, they can determine which ones will go on into the next decade and which should be enjoyed next Tuesday, but that's why they get paid the big bucks and I'm hauling boxes in someone else's house. Once again: you pay your money and you take your chances.

There is a product called the Perfect Sommelier that claims to age wines in just minutes. You place the open bottle on a powerful magnetic coaster and place a magnet over the top. I've tried it twice with differing results. For sure it does *something,* but I can't give it an outright endorsement except as the basis of neo-scientific experimentation. Nature does a better job.

Killing Your Children

I have a friend who has a "closet consultant." His job is to help people make sense of their wardrobe. The first thing this guy does is to throw out those neglected rags whose time, if there ever was a time for them, has now, sadly, passed. He does this, as they say in the legal profession, with prejudice. Picture Carson from *Queer Eye for the Straight Guy*. A typical consultation goes like this: "Out! Out! Out!" He says, "You may have some things in here which are debatable, but about these I will brook no argument. If you ever want to have the room for more clothes, the first step is the casting out of the infidels."

I'm Carson of the Wine Cellar. One of the interesting aspects of my job is that people, strangers, really, ask me to toss out bottles of inferior quality. I'm not a Master of Wine, but I can see what's what. I've had enough wine-by-the-glass at bars to know that if I ever see any of those titles in a "serious" cellar, it's time for me to chase them back from whence they came. Take your old Gamay Beaujolais to the local homeless shelter and get a tax deduction.

Sometimes I feel like a Forensic Oenologist, looking for clues in the matter of changing tastes. I see eleven bottles of old b-list Merlots slumming amid the riches of Bordeaux and Barolo, and I get a sense that the guy used to love this stuff when he first started collecting, but he's lost the taste for it. Imagine if you could only listen to the music you liked in college. My favorite group was the B-52s. I still love them, but I'm not dancing to *Rock Lobster* these days. It happens. Peoples' tastes mature and develop over time. They have more money now. It might still be okay juice, but it can't stand up to the competition.

People make mistakes along the way. They try a certain wine under certain circumstances, on their honeymoon trip to Italy for instance, sitting by the seaside, and the Pinot Grigio is perfect with the occasion, the setting, the sun dancing off the water, the Vespa, the Spaghetti alla Scoglio. They buy a case of the stuff. It doesn't travel. It has never been so far from home. It wasn't built to withstand the ravages of time. The next time the guy opens the honeymoon wine is on a damp and dreary winter's day and he harkens back to how he schlepped that box on the plane, through customs. He wonders what he was thinking.

There are the gift bottles that get shuffled to the bottom in the back of the cellar where they won't sully the good stuff up in front. Somebody, some well-meaning so-called friend, will give you a bottle of Jordan. Jordan is perfectly fine for bar wine. I applaud the tired, the poor, so righteous and everything, aspiring to breathe free and drink cheap, blah blah blah, but I have a responsibility to restore law and order. I feel like Clint Eastwood staring down some small time crook who's made the mistake of pulling out a Saturday night special to rob a corner grocery store on his beat. "Not in my cellar, punk."

So out goes the Jordan. Out go the nine-year-old Chardonnays, the six-dollar Merlot from Trader Joe's, the wicked and the weary. Out, out damn spot. I never actually, unilaterally, throw a client's wine out. I don't say, "Throw this crap in the garbage" because they may have a sentimental attachment to that bottle. What I do say is something to the effect of: "If you beg my pardon, sir, I can't help but notice that this wine does not appear to be up to the overall lofty standards of your cellar. If I may be permitted, I think your tastes have changed, and it appears that what you have here is a well-intentioned wine, which, if I may further impose, appears to be a bit hinky-dinky sir and, if I may add sir, you are not hinky-dinky."

I have a client in Connecticut who had a whole wall full of early nineties Chardonnays. No mid-nineties, which means he bought this stuff almost ten years ago and hasn't touched it. How do I know this? Because you can't find old Chardonnays in stores. You know why not? Because they're crap. They're not made that way. They don't have the structure. They're meant to be enjoyed early in the going. They're meant to be drunk within a year or two of their vintage date. Maybe four or five years. Some will hold up for a decade, but those are the "names," and this wasn't a "name." See ya.

One recent client called me the "Wine Nazi." Putting the unfortunate comparison to murderous fascists aside, he's dead right. I won't let you drink a Sauvignon Blanc from 1992. It's not a matter of taste, it's a matter of fact. You should constantly be improving your cellar.

Some guys can't let go. Either for sentimental reasons, or deep seated psychological reasons, they can't let go. Maybe they were the only child in their family, which would explain something about my father's collection. There are collectors who feel emotionally attached to each bottle, as though the merest hint that one might be substandard is like calling their children ugly. Well, buddy, if the shoe fits, your kids are butt ugly.

I just gave a big-time collector a list of twenty-five cases of junk. That adds up to about three percent of his holdings. Almost everyone could do to toss 3 to 5 percent of their collection. I used to work for a guy who prided himself on being the biggest asshole in town. At the company convention, he said that you should fire 5 percent of your workforce every year, just to keep the rest of the staff on their toes. Damn right! And don't let the door hit you on the way out.

During a maintenance session at a client's house in Las Vegas I pulled out eight titles, suggesting that they might be past their prime. The client asked me to stay for dinner and we'd see h how these bottles showed. The first one—a '93 Rabbit Ridge Zinfandel—still had some gas in the tank. Not a killer like the Turleys in his collection, and not something he'd pull out to impress a friend, but a decent bottle. I was sweating. What if I pulled out a bunch of not great but still good enough wines? I mean, just because I think something is substandard doesn't make it so. I'm happy to report that we threw the next five down the drain and my reputation remained intact for another day.

It is important to occasionally kill your children. I like to think of it as cellar rehabilitation. Your cellar is like your ball club. You may need to make some moves before the trading deadline if you want to make the playoffs this season. Your wine cellar is, at the heart of it, a real estate deal. You've only got so much room to work with. If you want to get more wine or better wine, you've got to make hard choices. This isn't Little League—not everybody gets to play.

What to do with wine that may not be good and may, in fact, be awful? I suggest you give it to someone who doesn't care. There are lots of people who don't care. They want to try something different. They don't mind tasting something bad, if only to know what bad tastes like. Connoisseurs, drunks, whatever. Simply say this: "We don't drink this wine anymore and, while I don't vouch for it, it might still be good." Then hand over a case of the crap and let it never darken your doorstep again.

Alternatively, my father and I like to have a bunch of people over to drink some old wines. Really old wines. Wines we suspect may have been at their peak during the first Bush administration. We round up people who can appreciate how great they were, the staying power of some, the unfortunate decline of others, the saying farewell to old friends aspect of it. Goodbye to all that, we say.

If you want to throw a farewell tasting, do a little prep. Get some pasta, some pate, some bread, some cheese and some salami, or buy something to go from an Italian restaurant. Set some dump buckets by the table, supply plenty of water, and give everyone three or four glasses with numbered stickers on them (this is going to save a lot of confusion when people who have been drinking for two hours want to know what's in the glass on the left. "Your left or my left?" Trust me, number the glasses with little stickers). Now pour away. Discuss each flight in turn. Ask a different person to lead the discussion each time. Ask for dissenting opinions. At one of these events, the best that could be said for a once-legendary Bordeaux was that it was, "redolent of the great vintage."

Selling It Off

Here's an old saw about buying wine as an investment: You want to know how to make a little money trading in wine? Start with a lot. Seriously, start with a *lot*. If you're buying wine as an investment, you've got to buy the best wines in full cases, in the original wood cases (OWC), from only the best vintages. DRC, Lafite, Petrus, Gaja. You buy them as futures (or you get on the mailing list), keep them in a temperature-controlled cellar for ten years or more, then you sell them for a huge profit with mercenary dispassion. You will recoup your investment, prove to the world what a savvy investor you are, and you will not have one drop of satisfaction to go with your winnings.

Another strategy follows along the same lines, but adds the "Pot Dealer Twist." Buy twice as much and sell off enough so you get the other half "for your head." Buy the assorted case of DRC, wait a while and then sell off the one bottle of Romanee-Conti. You should make enough on that to enjoy the other eleven bottles almost for free.

A lot of my clients take a look at their collections after they've been printed out in black and white and realize that they're long in one area. One client, a young guy in his early forties who has only been collecting for a few years, got too heavily into ports when he started out. I like port. I like it a lot. Fifty cases is a lot of port. Too much. So we are starting to weed it out. I worked out a barter deal with a retailer, who sold them some other wines to replace their ports. Retailers don't want your junk, but they're often short on older wines and are happy to make a deal if it's good stuff in good condition.

For other clients, we try to sell off wines that no longer fit in their cellar. This may be a result of changing tastes, a desire to upgrade, a loss of interest in one area, or to make room for an interest in something new. At least they get something to show for cleaning out their closet.

Selling wine has never been easier, thanks to Wine Bid (*www. winebid.com*) and Wine Commune (*www.winecommune.com*). Both services offer online auctions. Registration is free and they're very intuitive sites with tons of information, postings about wines, etc. They take a seller's commission of between 12 to 20 percent, depending on volume, and have very accurate, detailed accounting reports.

8

How to Enjoy
Your Wine Collection

The unfortunate thing about wine collecting is that too many people are too concerned with the prices or the ratings to let the wine flow. I think the most important thing is to enjoy yourself and let your wine collection be a conduit to good times. Dorothy J. Gaiter and John Brecher, the couple that writes the wine column for the *Wall Street Journal*, have started and popularized "Open That Special Bottle Day." Most of the time I think that reporting on fourteen dollar Sauvignon Blancs to the well heeled crowd reading the *Journal* misses the point, but on this they got it right.

A client of mine was planning a dinner party and had his chef call me to select the appropriate wines. The guests were Tom

Hanks, Larry David, Glenn Frey (of the Eagles) and their wives. I suggested that they start with champagne, Dom Perignon 1990, when the guests arrived, advising "and make sure everybody sees the label, that's half of what they're paying for." (This is both good advice and an accepted aspect of a proper wine service—you should always pour with the label facing your guests so they know what they're getting.) Then I suggested a white Burgundy with the first course and a red Bordeaux with the main course, in part because I knew my client had at least two bottles of each, in case somebody wanted more than one glass. Let me just add two things about this client: He's very rich and he's very wealthy. This is a spare-no-expenses lifestyle, with three homes, floor seats to the Lakers games, and what looks like a Mercedes dealership parked outside the door.

When I called back on Monday to see about the party, the chef sounded glum. "It was great," he said without enthusiasm.

"What about the wines?" I asked

"Well, Mrs. X said that stuff was too good, so she called the store and ordered some other wines and had them delivered."

They had an Oscar winner, an Emmy winner and a Grammy winner, but they were saving the good stuff for . . . whom, exactly? What are they waiting for? Other than the fact I've gotten a lot of mileage out of this story, it disgusts me.

The point is: You are going to die. You need to know this: you are going to die, so you should open the good stuff while you're still able. I wouldn't be surprised at all to find that my father's will begins with the phrase: "Being of sound mind and body, I drank the last of the La Tache this morning." Enjoy yourself; it's later than you think. (I now send this client postcards with notes that read: "For a good time, call Column Seventeen, Row G.")

Tastings & Wine Groups

Kurt Vonnegut once asked the painter Jasper Johns how you could tell a good picture. Johns said, "First, look at a million pictures." And so it is with wine.

My father (him again) has long been a member of a wine group called WOW, Wines of the World. They meet for lunch every other Friday, at a restaurant on Sunset Boulevard called Le Dome (the owner, Eddie Kerkhofs, is a member) since the dawn of time, around 1978. They are easily the most dysfunctional group of people I have ever had the pleasure to know. They've had deaths, divorces, and defections over the years. One member is either on the lam from the Feds or in the witness protection plan. Certain people won't sit on the same side of the table as certain other people. In other words, they're a family.

I would add that they're all richer for the time they've spent together and that the group, for all it's sniping, is actually good for the health of it's members. The average age of the WOW membership is now approaching 110, but they are, as one friend observed, "perfectly pickled and well preserved."

I recently started my own Friday lunch bunch with two other scions of the WOW legacy. Our first order of business was to come up with a name, but as nothing came to mind we called ourselves TBA as in To Be Announced or Trockenbeerenauslese. We brought Sam Denoff from the WOW group with us to the first official meeting. After listening to Sam weave stories of the olden, golden days of show business, one member of this new group turned to me and said, "This guy is fantastic. We've got to become geezers like them, drinking wine in the afternoon!" And so now we invite a geezer to lunch every time we get together. My father has been Geezer of the Month though he insists that he doesn't want to be known as a geezer, preferring instead the more genteel, respectful sound of Hall of Famer, or Veteran.

There are a couple of different ways of organizing a wine club, and it depends on the depth of the member's collections. I prefer the BYOB approach, with the caveat that "you will be judged by the company you keep." We quickly found that it's better to be as specific as possible, so rather than asking for an Italian wine we'll request members to bring a Barolo from '97 or earlier. Or pick a specific region and a year. Or try to piece together a vertical (the same wine in different years) among the members. (This will require quite a bit more hands-on management, and maybe more trouble than you want to deal with.)

MEMBERSHIP

The best things about a wine group are the unique relationships you develop with a group of people over a period of time. A wine club combines the empiricism of Ancient Rome, and the humor and bon-homie of twentieth-century drinking clubs, into a winey afternoon of liberté, égalité and fraternité. Membership to any group should be set at the highest possible standard. My father's other group, *Chazzers du Vin,* literally translated from the Yiddish as "Pigs of Wine," serves as a case in point. A friend of ours named David applied for membership to the group. The leader of the group said, "I don't think we have to review this man's character. He is a friend of ours and has been a regular guest of different members. I suggest we put this to a secret ballot." Each member was handed a slip of paper on which to cast their vote. The secretary of the club read the roll, and the final tally was twelve to one against. The stunned applicant called for a show of hands. The secretary said, "May I see who voted in favor of admission?" All thirteen members raised their hands.

If there is a lesson here, I don't know what it is. Half the fun of being a member in an elite group is derived from the camaraderie and fellowship of the group itself; the other half comes from rejecting others. Membership has its privileges.

Let me suggest a couple things if you're going to get into this at restaurants. First, go spend some time with the chef and/or the owner of the restaurant.

- You're going to want to have hors d'oeuvres and champagne or wine before you sit down.
- You're going to want to put together a menu that goes with your wines.*
- You may want to have more courses, in smaller proportions, served with flights of two to three wines to stretch them out.
- You're going to want to negotiate a favorable corkage policy.
- You may need a private room. (My Friday lunch bunch is so convivial, that most people don't like sitting near us.)
- You're going to want a rectangular table rather than a round table—better for conversation.
- You're going to want some or all of the wine decanted.
- You're going to need a lot of stemware.
- You want to make sure everything goes smoothly, that the restaurant has someone in charge of the whole production.
- You may want to sit outside if you plan to smoke.

....
* *There have been many inspired wine and food pairings over the years. Who can forget the dish of herring that was served with a flight of older Bordeaux? Or the tuna tartare with horseradish, paired with—some would argue that paired against is a more apt description—a vertical of Penfolds Grange? I'm not going to get too deep into the red-wine-with-fish debate here, but do be careful, it's a slippery slope.*

We put on a fantastic show at Spago recently with their beautiful sommelier Bonnie Graves at the helm. Everything flowed smoothly; the wines were poured precisely and delivered to the table like clockwork, ahead of each course. A month later, just down the street, we were struggling to get the wine poured by a guy who had been the busboy until we arrived with our bottles. They didn't know what to do with us.

The WOW group gets together at twelve-fifteen and ends around two-thirty, a nice, leisurely pace. Whenever I called my father at the office on Friday afternoons he was a little stoned-out. I wondered why he even pretended to go back to work after lunch with the boys, so I told my group to get their business done early on Friday so we can have a late lunch and knock off early. The pursuit of pleasure trumps the work ethic one Friday per month.

After our lunch at Spago, we went across the street to the Grand Havana Room for cigars and fifty-three-year-old port. (For the record, two is the maximum number of glasses of port one should ever undertake in one sitting.) One of the founding members of the TBA group got a cell phone call, pulled the phone out of his pocket, looked at it and let the call go to his voice mail. "Who was that?" I asked.

"It was my father," he said, "he works in the wine business. He was probably calling to see how lunch went."

"Why didn't you take the call?"

"Because it's six in the evening and I'm still at lunch!"

After that, the name of our group became the Coalition of the Willing.*

I try to find out, even at a BYOB event, what everyone is

....
*Among the Unwilling: One guy with a great collection quit the group after this lunch because not all of the others had wine nearly as good or, more to the point, as costly as what he brought. We bid him a fond adieu and went on with our lunch.

planning to bring with them, then make up a little Carte du Vin on my computer with the menu and the Parker and *Spectator* notes as the jumping off point for the ensuing discussion—which will hopefully evolve into a friendly argument, followed by name calling and threats of repercussions. When I had the temerity to suggest that I thought the 2001 Bryant Family Cabernet (a relatively meager 91 from RMP) was "a good wine," a writer friend demanded that I turn in my wine tasting credentials. I hastily added, "for a Syrah," which earned them back.

People like to play olfactory detective with the different scents you pick up in the bouquets of wines. Some are pretty farfetched: *"new* saddle shoes" (as opposed to old saddle shoes?), "crushed ants," "printer's ink" and, everybody's favorite, "barnyard." That's all well and good, but I think the real deal has more to do with how pleasurable the wine is, elements like balance, mouth-feel, concentration and finish, none of which have anything to do with dried fruits, cigar boxes or tar. These are sensations, not scents. There's more to wine than the semblance of raspberries.

At Home

Recently I took a journalist to a client's cellar. He took one look at the vast collection and asked, "How do you choose just one?" It's a good question. If you've got a '85 Romanee-Conti in the cellar, then drinking it is always a possibility, but you're probably not going to open such a wine with a pizza when you're home alone with the missus and Tivo. Pouring even a drop of this stuff down the drain is morally wrong, maybe even illegal in some states.

The answer is: you mix 'em up. One of the joys of having a cellar is that you have choices available to you. The only wrong decision is not going for the good stuff often enough. I have one client who is living life to the fullest in his hilltop palazzo, which houses a twelve-hundred bottle collection long on '82 Bordeaux and '90 Italians. That is, until company is coming over, when he gets a head count for the dinner party and runs out to the store to buy the wine. Another client complains that his three-thousand bottle cellar doesn't offer any everyday wine, whatever that is. I suggested (I don't *tell* my clients anything) that he should drink his '94 Araujo and '86 Latour as an everyday wine, not because there is anything everyday about it, but because he can. I *wish* this were my lament.

The debate continues on the subject of decanting wine, but I'm firmly in the Pro camp even at home. I decant my orange juice in the morning. With older wines you need to do it simply to get rid of the sediment in the bottom of the bottle. With younger wines, you'll want to do it to help open the wine up. (While I eschew any actual knowledge of Science, it is sometimes hard to avoid. By exposing the wine to air, you're advancing the maturation process. This is good to a point, then really, really bad. I went to a tasting at Christie's the other night where Anthony Hanson, the MW, admitted to having opened one bottle of Comte de Vogue Musigny 1991 too soon, so that it had faded by the time we finally tried it.)

Stand the wine up for at least an hour, ideally a full day before decanting, so the sediment settles at the bottom. In a recent mailer, Merus, a top Cabernet, suggests: "To fully enjoy the 2001 over the next twelve months, we recommend a *vigorous* decanting . . . and allow at least six hours of breathing time." Hold the wine over a light (a flashlight gives off more light, but a candle looks cooler) so you can see when the sediment starts to trickle down the length of the bottle as you pour it into the neck of the decanter. You may want to keep some cheesecloth around to get the most out of a bottle you haven't had a chance to stand up, or Ports that tend to get pretty gunky. There is a product called the *Wine Filter & Saver* that does a great job. Insert it into the neck of a wine bottle and a clever filtration system catches most of the sediment (*www.epicgifts.com*)

One nice thing about having a tasting at home is that you can set the atmosphere however you'd like with music and lighting. For comparative tastings, you may want to have dump buckets on the table. Most restaurants really frown on this. You don't want to clean any more glasses than you have to, and unless you're in a competitive tasting environment, good wines will rise above a reused glass.

One nice thing about going to a private house for a guys-only wine tastings is that you don't have to bring a gift. When I go out with my wife, we always bring a candle or chocolates as a hostess gift that invariably costs more than going out to dinner would have. Guys going to a wine tasting want to eat and drink and be left alone. They want to bring only their appetite, palate and opinions. They don't want to have to go shopping first.

GLASSES

One note about enjoying wine at home: get really good stemware. David Shaw in the *LA Times* said that "Virtually everyone who knows me knows that I am, shall we say, aesthetically challenged . . . but I love a beautiful wine glass." His short explanation: Good wine tastes better in good wine glasses. We held a tasting of the same wine poured into different glasses, and you really could tell the difference. His lengthier explanation: "The gentle curve of the bowl, the thin, elegant stem, the exquisite proportion . . . the angular line . . . " no wonder he won the Pulitzer Prize!

Riedel and Spieglau are pretty much the standard bearers. Riedel are a teensy bit more elegant and expensive, but Speiglau are more durable. Good glasses are not cheap, but they're not terribly expensive (both companies make a variety of product lines at different price points), so get two for every place seating and a couple more than that because you will break a few as you go. (There are a couple of glass-drying accessories that can help, somewhat, from Wine Enthusiast and IWA, among others.) I have four sets of glasses which have served me well: Champagne, Chardonnay, Bordeaux and Burgundy, although they offer a glass for almost every varietal under the sun.

By the way, it's called stemware because you're supposed to hold it by the stem. The one exception to this rule (and it is a Rule in my house) is when the wine is served too cold, then you are allowed to hold the bowl of the glass in your hands to warm it up a bit.

Riedel makes a tasting glass with a hollow stem that holds one ounce, enough for two sips, the "tasting" sip and the "confirming" sip. The glass is made of a kind of crystal that allows the wine to cling to the inside of the glass, revealing the color of the wine like you've never seen it before. And for whatever reason, the nose on the wine is more alive in that glass. I liked the tasting glass so much that I gave them to all my clients as holiday gifts.

If you want to put the theory that "You first taste with your eyes" to the test, Riedel makes an interesting all-black "blind tasting glass." A while back a newspaper article claimed that when wine was poured into a glass dark enough to mask the color, and served at a temperature cooler than room temperature but not ice-bucket cold, some wine experts couldn't even tell whether they were drinking white or red wine.

One note of caution that should come as a surprise to absolutely no one: wine is an alcoholic beverage. Part of its allure is its intoxicating quality. We call these evenings wine *tastings*, but there is a good deal of wine *drinking* that goes on. I recently attended a dinner with ten vintages of Bryant Family Cabernet, plus Champagne to start and a glass of Port with a cigar to wrap things up. That's a bottle of wine per person, spread out over five hours, and that cigar can kick your ass, too. Seriously, get a ride home. Take a cab. Hire a car. There's a new service in LA called Home James that sends a guy on a fold-up moped who drives you home in your own car. You don't need a DUI to cap off your evening.

Restaurants

I bring wine with me wherever I go. Most restaurants can't afford to cellar a lot of good wines, so their lists, while populated with notable names, offer only the latest vintages. I told one of my clients that he should take the wine carrying case I gave him, put one or two bottles of very good wine in it, and pay the corkage when he goes out to dinner. I suggested to him that he should offer a glass to the sommelier, send a glass back to the kitchen for the chef. "Do that, and you'll be getting a lot of free dessert." The client asked me to put this vital information into an e-mail memo and send it to him, so that his secretary could start the appropriate file. I told him I'd be happy to do so, because I think you have to take to this wine business in baby steps. I'm thrilled about the Charles Shaw phenomenon, Two-Buck Chuck. I think the wine is pretty dreary stuff (frankly, I'd rather drink muddy water), but for the same price as a six-pack, Joe Six-Pack and his wife might try a bottle of wine instead. If they like it, they might say, "I wonder what a six-dollar bottle of wine is like?" By the same token, if my client needs to start a file in order to bring his wine to the restaurant in order to get the free dessert, I'm happy to help.

Here's the rest of the memo: A couple notes about corkage: don't bring crap out in public—the restaurant won't think it's cute. If you're going to bring your own, make it worth the trip.

Play by the rules. Corkage costs what it costs. If it's ten dollars per bottle, you're getting off light. If it's twenty-five dollars per bottle, suck it up. Sona, a very good new restaurant in L.A., has a policy that allows you to bring one bottle for every two people. They explain that they don't make a lot of money on the food, and that we were eating into their profits by bringing our own. Fine. Bastide, another hot newcomer, doesn't allow you to bring outside wine and, as a result, some people simply don't go there. Vote with your pocketbook but don't complain about the house rules.

If you're planning to do a wine tasting meal at a restaurant, you can and should negotiate the corkage fee. Paying up to twenty-five dollars to bring a bottle out with you is not unreasonable, but paying hundreds in corkage is silly, especially if you're paying a premium for a set menu or a private room. Take care of the corkage up front, or you'll be in the unfortunate situation of trying to haggle with the restaurant manager after you've been drinking for three hours and all of your guests are getting restless waiting for you to resolve the check.

Get the wine to your lunch or dinner as early as possible, and set the order you want them poured, in flights if that is appropriate.

I like to decant the wine at home, rinse the bottle out and pour the wine back in, as taking a decanter to a restaurant can be incredibly impractical. I hope you will also put the cork back in the bottle before leaving the house, or suffer the consequences.

Finally, when you are bringing wine to a restaurant for a dinner or a tasting ask yourself whether wine goes better served with food from the same region, or if it just custom that makes us pair them together. I've heard this question answered differently. One school of thought suggests that the wine grew up with the food, so Italian wine's bracing acidity was meant to complement the tomato sauce common in Italian food. (James Orr, a writer who spun this theory adds, "Americans eat hamburgers, and we have 'hamburger wines.'") Some would argue that the new international "Parker" style of winemaking mitigates against these local and regional characteristics. Others would argue that if you bring good food, good wine and good people together, it doesn't matter where it came from.

Keeping Track: Wine Journal

A cellar book is a good idea. Keep track of the wines you've tasted, the meals they accompanied, the people who joined you.

I've started inputting tasting notes into my Excel spreadsheets. I select a cell and right-click on it. From the menu, select Insert Comment. I type in a line or two and close the comment cell, leaving a red flag in the corner of the cell as a reminder that a note exists. Pass the cursor over the flag and the notes reappear. You can also copy the Parker/*Spectator*/Tanzer notes into your sheets.

I have a *Festschrift*, a book that keeps track of dinner parties. It has a page for the menu, one for the seating chart, another for the wines served. You don't need a fancy book for this. There are plenty of nice blank books waiting for you at the stationery shop.

One friend puts the bottles in a warm water bath and peels off the labels with a safety razor blade at the end of the evening, then puts the labels into a composition notebook with the date.

Preserving Wine

Unfortunately, once you open the bottle and let the Genie out, it's a lot tougher getting the Genie back in.

If you find yourself with a half-a-bottle of wine leftover and you can't bear the thought of pouring the remainder down the drain, you should do one of the following:

- Pour the rest into a 375 ml bottle. The enemy is exposure to air. By shrinking the size of the bottle, you're limiting the amount of air it might come into contact with. Then put the bottle in the refrigerator overnight. (Forget what I said about constant temperature—in the matter of preserving flavors, cold is king.)
- Private Preserve is one of several preservation systems. A canister pumps nitrogen and other inert gasses down a long straw into the bottle (or decanter) "forming a protective gas on the wine's surface that blocks out the oxygen." Some people swear by it. I swear I can taste the gas. Then put the bottle in the refrigerator overnight.
- Stay up later and drink the rest of it.

9

Adventures in the Wine Trade

People who collect expensive, perishable things are a bit eccentric by nature, and because of that I meet a lot of interesting people in this business.

I have one client near San Diego who has assembled a cellar of more than ten thousand bottles, worth over five million dollars. He has it stored in a two-car garage. When I got there, the first room (capacity four thousand) was pretty full. He had built a second, larger room (capacity sixty five hundred) that was completely empty. Inside his house, in hundreds of shipper boxes were three thousand bottles of wine. The boxes were stacked shoulder-high, on either side of a forty-foot long corridor, running from the front door to the back of the house. The foyer, just inside the front door, was packed six-deep. We were stunned. We'd bring in five boxes at a time, unpack them, and go get more. Like the mythical beast Hydra, we'd cut off one head and two more would sprout up in the same place. The boxes reproduced like rabbits.

It took three of us three days to get it all put it all away in sections and counted. I made plans to go back down to finish up a couple weeks later, but the hallways had filled up again with almost one thousand new bottles. These weren't everyday, "good drinkin'" wines. These were '47 Cheval Blancs and Guigals by the armload. There was almost no room at the inn when we got down there, and now there were another eighty mixed cases looking for homes. Again, we got it all put away and nearly finished the count before we had to head back to L.A.

There were only two sections to go over, so again I made plans for a return trip to mop up. And again when I got down there, the foyer was jam packed with new arrivals. Now he'd gotten into Burgundy and, as Frank Sinatra sang, not in a shy way. There were '85s and '88s and '90s and '93s and '95s and '96s of Romanee-Conti in six and eight liter bottles. Other boxes revealed every great vintage of Petrus in every format imaginable. Out came Moutons from the '40s and Latours from the '20s. It was insane. Each bottle was a legend. I found myself laughing each time I tore open a new box, wondering what wonders lay inside.

Many of the wines were valued at over ten thousand dollars apiece. I'd made the mistake of pointing out that there was no Vega Sicilia in this great cellar, and now there was—lots and lots of it. There were Magnums of the legendary 1970 and every vintage before or since. I had to open my mouth. . . .

Last summer, I went out to a client's house in Valencia, north of the San Fernando Valley around six in the morning. The client has a hellish commute and tries to hit the road before the traffic gets too bad, so he showed me into the house, we talked about the cellar for a bit and he split before the rest of the family was even awake.

He has two adorable little kids, a five-year-old named Hannah and her three-year-old brother, Jake, who were on summer vacation. He told me to ignore them. Oh yeah, and there were a couple of cats I should ignore, too.

Easier said than done, it turned out. Hannah didn't have anyone to play with, and this new guy in the house (me) was the next best thing to a friend. Every ten minutes or so, she would come in to the little cellar (it was beautiful, but not very spacious for me, my assistant, two kids and a cat) and show me some Pokemon thing. She had books and cards and all kinds of collectible crap. Now, I love kids. I have a really good rapport with them. I also saw a fifteen-hour day ahead of me, and I was not looking forward to driving back out to Valencia if I didn't absolutely have to. I promised that would play together, later, then managed to ease her out of the cellar so we could get back to work. Around ten at night I finally gave in and sat down to play with her Pokemon cards. There's not much to this game, except knowing which ones are which. Fortunately for me I can read. I can even read upside down. This was very helpful, because I had no idea what was going on, and my five-year-old-friend could not read, at least not as well as I. "That's Morondo!" I said with confidence.

The Surreal Jigsaw Puzzle

Setting up a client's cellar is like putting a jigsaw puzzle together, except you don't know how many pieces there are or even what the picture looks like until you're done. You have to find every little piece of the puzzle, every bottle, before you can understand the nature of your client's collection. I came up with this jigsaw puzzle analogy when I was working in Westport, Connecticut last summer. I was pretty tired, so at the end of the day, I checked into a hotel and went up to my room, threw my bags down, spread out on the bed and turned on the TV. I was surprised to find that there was a jigsaw puzzle spread out on the little nightstand/desk. Part of the frame had been assembled, and other bits were sorted by color groupings in the top and bottom of the box on the table. I thought that maybe a jigsaw puzzle in every room was a signature of this hotel.

I started trying to connect some of the pieces with little success, and finally flipped over the cover to look at the picture. The scene depicted a cartoon drawing, but the joke was that the cover was only a *clue* as to what the real picture would be! I was working on a jigsaw puzzle but I would only know what I was trying to do once I was done. As I pondered this it hit me that a jigsaw puzzle is a pretty strange thing to have in a hotel room. They require a lot of time to complete, indoors, especially for tourists on summer vacation. The pieces are tiny and get lost easily. Not everyone likes them. The table was too small for a puzzle this size. I finally realized that the hotel had made a mistake and put me in somebody else's room. This puzzle was someone else's puzzle. I grabbed my bags and split, but I still remember the lesson of the puzzle to this day.

10

My Wedding Wines

I got married in the summer of 2003. My fiancée had a hundred questions for me about the floral arrangements, the rings, the Rabbi, the invitations, the band, the seat covers, the place settings, and various other arcane bits of wedding planning. The answer to all of them was "Honey, you decide." Under normal circumstances I would care, but I felt that recusing myself from the negotiations in these matters was actually problem solving. I gave in on almost everything in the name of insuring domestic tranquility. The wedding was going to be pretty much a show-up gig for me.

There was just one exception to this happy arrangement: food and wine. This was just too important to leave to my fiancée. My bride could eat a diet consisting solely of beige food. When we met, the only solid food in her refrigerator was hummus and string cheese. When we go out to restaurants, she usually looks at what I've ordered with that pathetic expression, like she might actually starve to death if she *can't just try* my steak instead of the listless, vegetable-based thing on her plate.

I have a client who has, through some fluke, fifty *cases* of '85 Margaux. His daughter is getting married this summer and I suggested that this sounds like a perfect opportunity to open a shit load of '85 Margaux. He disagreed, arguing that, at two hundred and fifty dollars a bottle (what it's worth now, not what he paid for it way back when), it was too expensive or too good for such a large gathering. He said he might serve the '98 Lynch Bages. (That is the same wine Jean Michel Cazes told my mother-in-law, "Sacre-bleu! You cannot open zees for at least five years.") What's the point? Is he going to have a bigger, better occasion to make a dent in this incredible cellar? The guy's fallback position, as I understand it, is to die and leave the wine to his daughter in his will. Then it will be her problem.

The first stirrings of trouble in my own wedding preparation started with the Rabbi. We went out to dinner with him to discuss the arrangements and Amy informed him that, "We want a traditional ceremony." What she meant to say was, "We don't want a traditional ceremony." He told us that there would be certain rituals, including the part where we drink twice from a Kiddush cup. The first sip represents our engagement, then some Hebrew stuff gets said, then the second sip symbolizes our marriage. I suggested that the wine be something extra special, perhaps the '83 Yquem. The Rabbi, a lovely guy, who was now going along with Amy's "traditional" theme insisted that we have a Kosher wine.

"They're not so bad," he said.

"That's the sales pitch? That's the best you can do?"

He didn't seem to see how this was an issue for me, a potential deal breaker in fact. I wasn't going to stop the wedding, but I seriously considered changing Rabbis. With less than a month to go we worked out a compromise: one cup of his sorry-ass Baron Herzog Chardonnay, and one cup of my '83 Yquem.

When the moment came, and he passed me the Kiddush cup, I instinctively sniffed, swirled and slurped. We all did. I barely let the Chardonnay past my lips and into my consciousness, but the Yquem was glorious. It was memorable. We saved the rest of the bottle to enjoy after dinner.

Having barely survived the ceremony, there was the party to consider. Let's bring my father back into the story. He had graciously offered me the run of his cellar for this occasion. Things got dicey as soon as he threw open the doors of the vault. What would your dream line-up be? No matter what team you select second-guessing is inevitable, after all, if you put Willie Mays in Center Field that means leaving Mickey Mantle off the team. I knew exactly what he had; he was my first client, after all. His collection is broader than it is deep. He has a wide array of '82 Bordeaux, for example, but not as many as six of any one title. We needed about six bottles of two different red wines, plus '90 Dom Perignon and a serviceable white Burgundy for the fish course.

For years now my father has allocated front and center display space in his cellar to an imperial (six liters) of 1961 Lafite. Only a few of its kind are still in existence. He is very clear that if we don't drink this bottle during his lifetime he wants us to put it in the casket next to him, or pour it over him, because he is determined to prove the pundits wrong and take it with him. His son's wedding seems like the kind of occasion he must have pictured when he bought that bottle. The problem is that we were having a small wedding, thirty-five people including many who don't drink or don't know or don't care. People we have learned to love despite these character flaws. The imperial was eight bottles in one, almost certainly too much wine—and you'd have to cry over pouring '61 Lafite down the drain—regardless of Mr. Parker's unfortunate experience with this wine. I was trying to explain this problem to some of my vinous friends from the Coalition of the Willing. Two of them volunteered to wait tables at the wedding. "We'll come in and clean up for you."

What are friends for?

Would the characteristics of a somewhat older Burgundy (Leroy Vosne Romanee Cros Parantoux '91) be wasted on these heathens who are my new family? Probably. We imagined the horror of my father-in-law adding an ice cube. Same goes for the Conterno Granbussia Barolo '90. Too precious, perhaps?

In the end we decided it was better to get a fastball down the middle of the plate. We settled (if you can call it that) on the '89 Gaja Sori San Lorenzo with the pasta course, and the '89 La Mission Haut Brion with the filet.

I'm happy to report that the marriage is holding and we just had our first child.

Appendix A: Sites

The Internet has done more for wine knowledge and wine sales than . . . everything that came before it. You can now find out just about everything, if you know where to look. If you don't know where to look, Google does. A list of some of my favorite wine Web sites follows below, but there are tons more of them, and I love finding out about new ones with different approaches to the subject. Most of the sites listed below have some overlap—everyone sells accessories, there are all kinds of events going on.

All of the sites listed below (and a few more) can also be found online at *www.thebestcellar.com/links*.

Subscription Sites

- *www.erobertparker.com* In a word: Indispensable.
- *www.winespectator.com* The layout isn't great and I've already subscribed to their weekly newsletter—but that doesn't stop the pop-up *every time* I log on. Otherwise, very worthwhile.
- *www.iwc.com* Tanzer's International Wine Cellar page.
- *www.burghound.com* Alan Meadows' Burgundy-only subscription e-mag. I think you're better off with the print version.

Wine Prices

- *www.winesearcher.com*
- *www.winemarketjournal.com*
- *www.vines.org*

Auction Sites

Online Auctions

- Wine Bid *www.winebid.com*
- Wine Commune *www.winecommune.com*
- Brentwood Wine *www.brentwoodwine.com*

Auction Houses

- Zachy's *www.zachys.com*
- Christies *www.christies.com*
- Bonhams & Butterfields *www.bonhams.com*
- Sotheby's *www.sothebys.com*
- Morrel & Co. *www.morrel.com*
- The Chicago Wine Company *www.tcwc.com*
- Hart Davis Hart *www.hdhwine.com*
- Acker, Merrall & Condit *www.ackerwines.com*

Online Inventory Management

- *www.cellartracker.com*
- *www.vinfolio.com*

Winemaker Sites

There are too many winemaker sites to list, so get the list from:
- *www.winostuff.com/winery_links.htm*

Educational Sites

- Wine Business Magazine *www.winebusiness.com*
- Local Wine Events *www.localwineevents.com* Tons of opportunity, much of it crap, for the avid taster.

- *www.intowine.com* Lots of interesting factoids, including every biblical reference to wines and vines.
- Wine Institute *www.wineinstitute.org* State laws for shipping, lots of interesting industry stats.
- *www.wineloverspage.com* Robin Garr has a very inclusive, entertaining site.
- *www.winereader.com* Well organized site of wine books links to amazon.com.

Accessories & Glasses

- The Wine Enthusiast *www.wineenthusiast.com*
- International Wine Accessories *www.iwa.com*
- Wine Jazz *www.winejazz.com*
- *www.winehome.com*
- *www.finelycorked.com*
- Riedel *www.riedelcrystal.com* and
- Spieglau *www.spieglau.com* Both sites have links to local dealers, but neither has prices.
- Amazon *www.amazon.com* They've got everything.

Wine Racks

There are quite a few wine rack sites available, these are two of the best:
- *www.wineracks.com*
- *www.winecellarinnovations.com*

Wine Cellar Builders

- Cellar Masters *www.cellarmastersinc.com*
- Cellar Works *www.cellarworks.com*

- Wine Cellar Concepts *www.winecellarconcepts.com*

Online Stores

In alphabetical order:

- 20-20 *www.2020wine.com*
- Antique Wine Co. *www.antiquewineco.com*
- Brown Derby *www.brownderby.com*
- Garagiste *www.garagiste.com*
- John and Pete's *www.johnandpetes.com*
- John Hart Fine Wine *www.johnhart.com*
- K and L Wines *www.klwines.com*
- *www.kosherwine.com* (if you really must—frankly, I think it best to simply renounce your faith, heritage, thousands of years of history and buy non-kosher wine, but that's just me.)
- Premier Cru *www.premiercru.com*
- Prime Wine *www.primewine.com*
- Rare Wine Company *www.rarewineco.com*
- Sam's Wine *www.samswine.com*
- Sherry Lehmann *www.sherry-lehmann.com*
- D. Sokolin *www.sokolin.com*
- Superior Wine *www.superiorwine.com*
- Wally's *www.wallywine.com*
- Wine.com *www.wine.com*
- The Wine Broker *www.thewinebroker.com*
- Wine Club *www.thewineclub.com*
- The Wine Exchange *www.winex.com*
- The Wine House *www.winehouse.com*
- The Wine Messenger *www.winemessenger.com*
- Woodland Hills Wine Company *www.whwc.com*
- Zachy's *www.zachys.com*

Appendix B: Wine Books

Parker's Wine Buyer's Guide, Robert M. Parker, Simon & Schuster 2002. At 1,635 pages it is a lot more than you wanted to know, but it is the Bible.

The Wine Bible, Karen MacNeil, Workman 2001. The best survey book I've read.

Bacchus and Me, Jay McInerny, Vintage 2002. A plain speaking collection of his stories for House & Garden magazine.

Red Wine With Fish, Joshua Wesson and David Rosengarten, Simon & Schuster 1989.

Making Sense of Burgundy, Matt Kramer, William Morrow 1990.

Exploring Wine, Steven Kolpan, Brian H. Smith & Michael A. Weiss, Wiley 2001.

Wines of France (Third Edition, Revised), Alexis Lichine, Knopf (The original edition was published in 1951. At around 320 pages, my 1960 edition states modestly on its cover, "Not only the most comprehensive, but far and away the best book on its subject that has ever been written in any language."

The Great Vintage Wine Book, Michael Broadbent (Broadbent was head of the Wine Department at Christie's in the UK for years, and one of the most knowledgeable writers on wine in the era BP, Before Parker. His five-star scoring system now seems so quaint, so anachronistic—as does Clive Coates' twenty-point scale. I don't think you're going to see wine ratings get "Two thumbs up!" any time soon. The 100-point curve is here to stay.)

Bordeaux, Robert Parker, Dorling Kindersley 2003.

Gambero Rosso, Daniele Cernilli and Carlo Petrini, Grafe & Unzer 2003.

Jancis Robinson's Wine Course, Jancis Robinson, Abbeville Press 1996.

How and Why to Build a Wine Cellar, Richard M. Gold, Ph. D., Sandhill Publishers 1996. (Dreary prose, but good advice for those hearty, foolish souls who endeavor to do it themselves.)

Cellaring Wine, Jeff Cox, Storey Publishing 2003.

Making Sense of Wine, Matt Kramer, Running Press, 2003.

Noble Rot, William Echikson, W.W. Norton, 2004.

Hugh Johnson's World Atlas of Wine, Simon and Schuster 1971.